elevate science

SAVVAS
LEARNING COMPANY

You are an author!

This is your book to keep. Write and draw in it! Record your data and discoveries in it! You are an author of this book!

Print your name, school, town, and state below.

My Photo

Name_____

School_____

Town, State_____

ISBN-13:   978-0-328-94874-1
ISBN-10:   0-328-94874-8
12   22

Program Authors

ZIPPORAH MILLER, EdD

Coordinator for K-12 Science Programs, Anne Arundel County Public Schools.
Zipporah Miller currently serves as the Senior Manager for Organizational Learning with the Anne Arundel County Public School System. Prior to that she served as the K-12 Coordinator for science in Anne Arundel County. She conducts national training to science stakeholders on the Next Generation Science Standards. Dr. Miller also served as the Associate Executive Director for Professional Development Programs and conferences at the National Science Teachers Association (NSTA) and served as a reviewer during the development of Next Generation Science Standards. Dr, Miller holds a doctoral degree from University of Maryland College Park, a master's degree in school administration and supervision from Bowie State University, and a bachelor's degree from Chadron State College.

MICHAEL J. PADILLA, PhD

Professor Emeritus, Eugene P. Moore School of Education, Clemson University, Clemson, South Carolina
Michael J. Padilla taught science in middle and secondary schools, has more than 30 years of experience educating middle grades science teachers, and served as one of the writers of the 1996 U.S. National Science Education Standards. In recent years Mike has focused on teaching science to English Language Learners. His extensive leadership experience, serving as Principal Investigator on numerous National Science Foundation and U.S. Department of Education grants, resulted in more than $35 million in funding to improve science education. He served as president of the National Science Teachers Association, the world's largest science teaching organization, in 2005–6.

MICHAEL E. WYSESSION, PhD

Professor of Earth and Planetary Sciences, Washington University, St. Louis, Missouri
An author on more than 100 science and science education publications, Dr. Wysession was awarded the prestigious National Science Foundation Presidential Faculty Fellowship and Packard Foundation Fellowship for his research in geophysics, primarily focused on using seismic tomography to determine the forces driving plate tectonics. Dr. Wysession is also a leader in geoscience literacy and education, including being chair of the Earth Science Literacy Principles, author of several popular geology Great Courses video lecture series, and a lead writer of the Next Generation Science Standards*.

Reviewers

Program Consultants

Carol Baker
Science Curriculum

Dr. Carol K. Baker is superintendent for Lyons Elementary K-8 School District in Lyons, Illinois. Prior to that, she was Director of Curriculum for Science and Music in Oak Lawn, Illinois. Before that she taught Physics and Earth Science for 18 years. In the recent past, Dr. Baker also wrote assessment questions for ACT (EXPLORE and PLAN), was elected president of the Illinois Science Teachers Association from 2011-2013 and served as a member of the Museum of Science and Industry advisory boards in Chicago. She is a writer of the Next Generation Science Standards. Dr. Baker received her BS in Physics and a science teaching certification. She completed her Master of Educational Administration (K-12) and earned her doctorate in Educational Leadership.

Jim Cummins
ELL

Dr. Cummins's research focuses on literacy development in multilingual schools and the role technology plays in learning across the curriculum. *Elevate Science* incorporates research-based principles for integrating language with the teaching of academic content based on Dr. Cummins's work.

Elfrieda Hiebert
Literacy

Dr. Hiebert is the President and CEO of TextProject, a nonprofit aimed at providing open-access resources for instruction of beginning and struggling readers, and a former primary school teacher. She is also a research associate at the University of California Santa Cruz. Her research addresses how fluency, vocabulary, and knowledge can be fostered through appropriate texts, and her contributions have been recognized through awards, such as the Oscar Causey Award for Outstanding Contributions to Reading Research (Literacy Research Association, 2015), Research to Practice Award (American Educational Research Association, 2013), William S. Gray Citation of Merit Award for Outstanding Contributions to Reading Research (International Reading Association, 2008).

Content Reviewers

Alex Blom, Ph.D.
Associate Professor
Department Of Physical Sciences
Alverno College
Milwaukee, Wisconsin

Joy Branlund, Ph.D.
Department of Physical Science
Southwestern Illinois College
Granite City, Illinois

Judy Calhoun
Associate Professor
Physical Sciences
Alverno College
Milwaukee, Wisconsin

Stefan Debbert
Associate Professor of Chemistry
Lawrence University
Appleton, Wisconsin

Diane Doser
Professor
Department of Geological Sciences
University of Texas at El Paso
El Paso, Texas

Rick Duhrkopf, Ph. D.
Department of Biology
Baylor University
Waco, Texas

Jennifer Liang
University Of Minnesota Duluth
Duluth, Minnesota

Heather Mernitz, Ph.D.
Associate Professor of Physical Sciences
Alverno College
Milwaukee, Wisconsin

Joseph McCullough, Ph.D.
Cabrillo College
Aptos, California

Katie M. Nemeth, Ph.D.
Assistant Professor
College of Science and Engineering
University of Minnesota Duluth
Duluth, Minnesota

Maik Pertermann
Department of Geology
Western Wyoming Community College
Rock Springs, Wyoming

Scott Rochette
Department of the Earth Sciences
The College at Brockport
 State University of New York
Brockport, New York

David Schuster
Washington University in St Louis
St. Louis, Missouri

Shannon Stevenson
Department of Biology
University of Minnesota Duluth
Duluth, Minnesota

Paul Stoddard, Ph.D.
Department of Geology and
 Environmental Geosciences
Northern Illinois University
DeKalb, Illinois

Nancy Taylor
American Public University
Charles Town, West Virginia

Safety Reviewers

Douglas Mandt, M.S.
Science Education Consultant
Edgewood, Washington

Juliana Textley, Ph.D.
Author, NSTA books on school
 science safety
Adjunct Professor
Lesley University
Cambridge, Massachusetts

Teacher Reviewers

Jennifer Bennett, M.A.
Memorial Middle School
Tampa, Florida

Sonia Blackstone
Lake County Schools
Howey In the Hills, Florida

Teresa Bode
Roosevelt Elementary
Tampa, Florida

Tyler C. Britt, Ed.S.
Curriculum & Instructional
 Practice Coordinator
Raytown Quality Schools
Raytown, Missouri

A. Colleen Campos
Grandview High School
Aurora, Colorado

Coleen Doulk
Challenger School
Spring Hill, Florida

Mary D. Dube
Burnett Middle School
Seffner, Florida

Sandra Galpin
Adams Middle School
Tampa, Florida

Margaret Henry
Lebanon Junior High School
Lebanon, Ohio

Christina Hill
Beth Shields Middle School
Ruskin, Florida

Judy Johnis
Gorden Burnett Middle School
Seffner, Florida

Karen Y. Johnson
Beth Shields Middle School
Ruskin, Florida

Jane Kemp
Lockhart Elementary School
Tampa, Florida

Denise Kuhling
Adams Middle School
Tampa, Florida

Esther Leonard M.Ed. and L.M.T.
Gifted and Talented Implementation Specialist
San Antonio Independent School District
San Antonio, Texas

Kelly Maharaj
Science Department Chairperson
Challenger K8 School of Science and
 Mathematics
Elgin, Florida

Kevin J. Maser, Ed.D.
H. Frank Carey Jr/Sr High School
Franklin Square, New York

Angie L. Matamoros, Ph.D.
ALM Science Consultant
Weston, Florida

Corey Mayle
Brogden Middle School
Durham, North Carolina

Keith McCarthy
George Washington Middle School
Wayne, New Jersey

Yolanda O. Peña
John F. Kennedy Junior High School
West Valley City, Utah

Kathleen M. Poe
Jacksonville Beach Elementary School
Jacksonville Beach, Florida

Wendy Rauld
Monroe Middle School
Tampa, Florida

Bryna Selig
Gaithersburg Middle School
Gaithersburg, Maryland

Pat (Patricia) Shane, Ph.D.
STEM & ELA Education Consultant
Chapel Hill, North Carolina

Diana Shelton
Burnett Middle School
Seffner, Florida

Nakia Sturrup
Jennings Middle School
Seffner, Florida

Melissa Triebwasser
Walden Lake Elementary
Plant City, Florida

Michele Bubley Wiehagen
Science Coach
Miles Elementary School
Tampa, Florida

Pauline Wilcox
Instructional Science Coach
Fox Chapel Middle School
Spring Hill, Florida

2-PS1-1, 2-PS1-2, K-2-ETS1-1, K-2-ETS1-2

Properties of Matter

Quest

In this Quest activity, you meet a toy engineer. She needs your help. She wants you to choose materials for a toy kit that kids will use to make model buildings.

Like the toy engineer, you will complete activities and labs. You will use what you learn in the lessons to choose materials for a model building kit. Then you can try to make the kit.

Find your Quest activities on pages 11, 19, 24, and 32.

Career Connection Toy Engineer on page 35

- VIDEO
- eTEXT
- INTERACTIVITY
- SCIENCE SONG
- GAME
- DOCUMENT
- ASSESSMENT

HANDS-ON LAB

Topic 2

2-PS1-1, 2-PS1-3, 2-PS1-4

Changing Matter

Quest

In this Quest activity, you meet a structural engineer. She is building a bridge. She wants you to help her choose the best materials for the bridge.

Like the structural engineer, you will complete activities and labs. You will use what you learn in the lessons to choose materials for a bridge. Then you will explain your choices in a letter.

Find your Quest activities on pages 53, 59, and 64.

Career Connection Engineer on page 69

- ▶ VIDEO
- 📖 eTEXT
- 👆 INTERACTIVITY
- ▶ SCIENCE SONG
- 🎮 GAME
- 📄 DOCUMENT
- ☑ ASSESSMENT

The Essential Question

HANDS-ON LAB

Topic 3

2-ESS2-1, 2-ESS2-2, 2-ESS2-3, K-2-ETS1-3

Earth's Water and Land

In this Quest activity, you meet a map maker. She needs your help. She is making a map for hikers going on a scavenger hunt. She will draw landforms and bodies of water on the map.

Like a map maker, you will complete activities and labs. You will use what you learn in the lessons to design a map for hikers. Then you will make your map.

Find your Quest activities on pages 88, 95, and 102.

Career Connection Map Maker on page 105

▶ VIDEO

📖 eTEXT

👆 INTERACTIVITY

▶ SCIENCE SONG

🎮 GAME

📄 DOCUMENT

☑ ASSESSMENT

HANDS-ON LAB

Topic 4

Earth's Processes

2-ESS1-1, 2-ESS2-1, K-2-ETS1-3

Quest

In this Quest activity, you meet an environmental engineer. She needs your help. The ocean is slowly washing away the coastline near a small town. She wants to design a way to stop it from happening.

Like an environmental engineer, you will complete activities and labs. You will use what you learn in the lessons to find a solution to coastline erosion. You will test your solution and compare your data with that obtained from tests of other solutions.

Find your Quest activities on pages 123, 128, and 136.

Career Connection Environmental Engineer on page 141

▶ VIDEO

📖 eTEXT

👆 INTERACTIVITY

▶ SCIENCE SONG

🎮 GAME

📄 DOCUMENT

☑ ASSESSMENT

HANDS-ON LAB

Plants and Animals

Quest

In this Quest activity, you meet a botanist. He needs help taking care of a plant called *Rafflesia arnoldii*, or the corpse lily. He would like you to help him write about ways to care for the plant.

Like the botanist, you will complete activities and labs. You will use what you learn in the lessons to write a guidebook that describes how to care for the corpse lily.

Find your Quest activities on pages 161, 166, 172, and 178.

Career Connection Botanist on page 183

▶	VIDEO
📖	eTEXT
👆	INTERACTIVITY
▶	SCIENCE SONG
🎮	GAME
📄	DOCUMENT
☑	ASSESSMENT

The Essential Question

HANDS-ON LAB

Topic 6

Habitats

Quest

In this Quest activity, you meet an ecologist. He would like you to help him make a presentation to city officials. He wants you to explain why the city needs to protect a local habitat.

Like the ecologist, you will complete activities and labs. You will use what you learn in the lessons to make a presentation about a habitat.

Find your Quest activities on pages 200, 209, and 216.

Career Connection Ecologist on page 219

- ▶ VIDEO
- 📖 eTEXT
- ☝ INTERACTIVITY
- ▶ SCIENCE SONG
- 🎮 GAME
- 📄 DOCUMENT
- ☑ ASSESSMENT

The Essential Question

HANDS-ON LAB

Elevate your thinking!

Elevate Science takes science to a whole new level and lets you take ownership of your learning. Explore science in the world around you. Investigate how things work. Think critically and solve problems! *Elevate Science* helps you think like a scientist, so you're ready for a world of discoveries.

Explore Your World

Explore real-life scenarios with engaging Quests that dig into science topics around the world. You can:

- Solve real-world problems
- Apply skills and knowledge
- Communicate solutions

Make Connections

Elevate Science connects science to other subjects and shows you how to better understand the world through:

- Mathematics
- Reading and Writing
- Literacy

Quest Kickoff

Find the Parents

What clues help us find a young animal's parent?

Literacy ▸ Toolbox

Main Ideas and Details All living things grow and change is the main idea. Use the details to tell how a watermelon plant changes during its life cycle.

Math ▸ Toolbox

Compare Numbers
You can compare how long objects are. Parent rabbits have longer ears than young rabbits. Use cubes to measure the lengths of two classroom objects. Which is longer?

Connecting Concepts ▸ Toolbox

Patterns Nature has many patterns. A **pattern** is something that repeats. Parents protect their young. They use their bodies to protect them. What patterns do you see on these two pages?

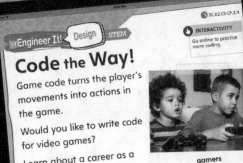

On tablet screen:

Engineer It! Design **STEM**   SC.K2.CS-CP.2.4

INTERACTIVITY
Go online to practice more coding.

Code the Way!
Game code turns the player's movements into actions in the game.

Would you like to write code for video games?

Learn about a career as a software engineer.

gamers

Design It

Build Skills for the Future

- Master the Engineering Design Process
- Apply critical thinking and analytical skills
- Learn about STEM careers

Focus on Reading Skills

Elevate Science creates ongoing reading connections to help you develop the reading skills you need to succeed. Features include:

- Leveled Readers
- Literacy Connection Features
- Reading Checks

Literacy Connection

Main Idea and Details

Nature scientists observe animals. Read about the main idea and details of geese and their young.

The main idea is what the sentences are about. Details tell about the main idea.

GAME
Practice what you learn with the Toolbox Games.

Enter the Lab

Hands-on experiments and virtual labs help you test ideas and show what you know in performance-based assessments. Scaffolded labs include:

- STEM Labs
- Design Your Own
- Open-ended Labs

On tablet screen:

Alike and Different: Living Things

Click the pictures. Compare how living things and their parents are alike and different. Write your answer below.

Type your answer here.

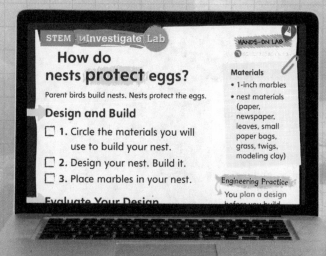

On laptop screen:

STEM ₁Investigate **Lab**   **HANDS-ON LAB**

How do nests protect eggs?

Parent birds build nests. Nests protect the eggs.

Design and Build

☐ 1. Circle the materials you will use to build your nest.

☐ 2. Design your nest. Build it.

☐ 3. Place marbles in your nest.

Evaluate Your Design

Materials
- 1-inch marbles
- nest materials (paper, newspaper, leaves, small paper bags, grass, twigs, modeling clay)

Engineering Practice
You plan a design before you build

Engineering Practice
You plan a design before you build something.

⚠ **Wash your hands when you are done.**

Properties of Matter

Next Generation Science Standards

2-PS1-1 Plan and conduct an investigation to describe and classify different kinds of materials by their observable properties.

2-PS1-2 Analyze data obtained from testing different materials to determine which materials have the properties that are best suited for an intended purpose.

K-2-ETS1-1 Ask questions, make observations, and gather information about a situation people want to change to define a simple problem that can be solved through the development of a new or improved object or tool.

K-2-ETS1-2 Develop a simple sketch, drawing, or physical model to illustrate how the shape of an object helps it function.

Go online to access
your digital course.

▶ VIDEO

📖 eTEXT

👆 INTERACTIVITY

▶ SCIENCE SONG

🎮 GAME

☑ ASSESSMENT

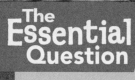

The Essential Question How can different materials be used?

Show What You Know

Look at the picture. How can the materials be used?

Topic 1   Properties of Matter   1

Toy Building Kit

Why do we use different materials for a toy kit?

Phenomenon Hi! I am Dr. Ayashi. I am a toy engineer. I study materials to make toys. I also test toys. I want them to be safe. I want them to last a long time.

I need to design a kit for kids to make model buildings. Help me pick objects for the kit. Observe and test objects. Keep track of your observations in a chart. The path shows the Quest activities you will complete. Check off your progress each time you complete an activity with a **QUEST CHECK ✓ OFF** .

Quest Check-In 1

Lesson 1 ▪

Use what you learned to classify objects as solid, liquid, or gas. Decide if the objects are good for building.

Next Generation Science Standards

2-PS1-2 Analyze data obtained from testing different materials to determine which materials have the properties that are best suited for an intended purpose.

K-2-ETS1-1 Ask questions, make observations, and gather information about a situation people want to change to define a simple problem that can be solved through the development of a new or improved object or tool.

Quest Check-In Lab 3

Lesson 3 ◆

Use what you learned
about the properties of
blocks to build something.

Quest Check-In 2

Lesson 2 ●

Use what you learned about
properties of matter. Observe
and classify building blocks.

Quest Check-In 4

Lesson 4 ▲

Use what you learned
about liquids and gases.
Explain if you could use
liquids and gases in
the kit.

Quest Findings

Complete the Quest! Use your
chart. Describe what materials
you would include in the toy
building kit.

uConnect Lab

HANDS-ON LAB

2-PS1-2, SEP.3, SEP.4

Which object is **bigger?**

Engineers observe the materials they use. They also measure them. How do you know one object is bigger than another?

Materials

- two objects

Suggested Materials

- ruler
- connecting blocks
- paperclips

Procedure

☐ **1.** Look at two objects. Think of how you can show which is bigger. Make a plan to investigate.

☐ **2.** Measure the objects. **Collect data.**

Science Practice

You measure to collect data.

Observations	

Analyze and Interpret Data

3. Circle data that show which object is bigger. Underline data that show which object is smaller.

4. Tell how you know which object is bigger.

4   **Topic 1   Properties of Matter**

Cause and Effect

GAME

Practice what you learn with the Mini Games.

An engineer may need to test materials. One test could include magnets. Read about the causes and effects of using magnets on different materials.

A cause makes something happen. An effect is the result.

Magnets

You want to test if materials are magnetic. Materials are magnetic if they are able to be pushed or pulled by a magnet. You place a magnet on the back of a plastic chair. The magnet does not stick. Next, you put the magnet on the metal leg of the chair. The magnet sticks to the leg of the chair! The metal leg is magnetic. The plastic seat is not.

✓ Reading Check Cause and Effect

Underline what causes a magnet to stick. Circle the effect that plastic has on a magnet.

plastic chair with metal legs

Describe Matter

Vocabulary

matter

solid

liquid

gas

properties

I can tell the difference between a solid, a liquid, and a gas.

2-PS1-1

Jumpstart Discovery!

Look around. What are some different objects that you see? Describe an object to a partner. Ask your partner to guess the object.

What is **different?**

Life scientists sort plants and animals based on their features. How can you sort objects?

Procedure

☐ 1. **Observe** six objects.

☐ 2. Sort the objects at least three different ways. Use the features of the objects to help you decide.

Analyze and Interpret Data

3. How did you sort the objects?

_____

_____

_____

_____

4. How did another group sort differently?

_____

_____

_____

_____

Suggested Materials

- cup
- book
- eraser
- calculator
- ball
- water
- magnet
- letters

Science Practice

You **observe** when you look closely at things.

VIDEO

Watch a video about describing matter.

Matter Everywhere

Look around you. Everything you can see, touch, or smell is made up of matter. **Matter** is anything that has weight and takes up space. A desk is made of matter. A chair is made of matter. Everything is made up of matter even if you cannot tell it is there.

paint

To describe matter, you observe its properties. **Properties** are the traits or features of an object. Color, shape, and size are properties.

Identify Circle matter that is blue.

Explain How do you know if something is matter?

Types of Matter

INTERACTIVITY

Complete an activity on classifying matter.

A **solid** is matter that has its own size and shape. A **liquid** is matter that does not have its own shape. A **gas** is matter that does not have its own shape or size. Liquids and gases take the shape of their containers.

The balls are all solid. Some are made of rubber, plastic, or fabric. Some of the balls are filled with air. Air is made of gases.

soccer ball

Observe Look at the balls in the pictures. Circle the largest ball. Place an X on the smallest ball.

tennis ball

football

☑ **Reading Check** Cause and Effect

A ball is being filled with air. Tell what you think the effect is on the ball's shape.

basketball

Describe Matter

Some properties you can observe with your senses. You can measure other properties.

Think about liquid water and frozen water. Water is a liquid. An ice cube is frozen water. It is a solid. The ice cube is cold. Liquid water can be cool, warm, or hot. You can measure their temperatures.

Literacy ▸ Toolbox

Cause and Effect If you freeze water, what is the effect? What would cause an ice cube to turn back into liquid water?

Quest Connection

Could you use ice cubes to build a toy house in a warm room? Why or why not?

Label each item as a solid, liquid, or gas.

liquid

solid

gas

Build with Solids, Liquids, and Gases

Some objects do a job better than others. You can observe the properties of an object. You can see if the object would be good for a job.

Object			
Type of Matter			
Properties			
Useful for Building			

Collect Data Classify objects as solid, liquid, or gas. Record your data in the chart. What objects would you put in your kit? Why?

uEngineer It! Model STEM

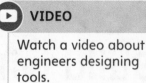
VIDEO
Watch a video about engineers designing tools.

Design a Nutcracker!

Phenomenon Nutcrackers are tools. People use nutcrackers to open the hard shells of nuts.

Some animals also eat nuts. The tools they use can be part of their bodies. Birds use their beaks. Squirrels use teeth to crack nuts. Some animals bang the nut to open it. Some animals drop the nuts from high above to try to break them open.

Look at the pictures of these animals.

ground squirrel

parrot

CCC Structure and Function The animals eat nuts and hard seeds. What do you notice about their mouths?

Model It

Nutcrackers are usually made from hard, strong materials. They must be easy to hold. They must be hard enough to crack a nut. How can you make a nutcracker by modeling after the animals?

☐ Draw a design of your model nutcracker.

☐ Label the materials used in each part of the nutcracker.

☐ Share your design. Compare it to another design.

☐ Tell how you could improve your design.

Properties of Matter

Vocabulary

weight
texture
magnetic
flexibility
hardness

I can describe matter by its properties.

_____

2-PS1-1

Jumpstart Discovery!

Look at the dam. What slows down the flow of the water? Discuss with a partner.

HANDS-ON LAB
2-PS1-2, K-2-ETS1-2, SEP.2

What can beavers teach engineers?

Engineers can learn from nature. Beavers build dams to change the flow of water. Engineers also build dams. How can you change the way water flows?

Materials
- plastic bin
- water

Suggested Materials
- craft sticks
- glue
- modeling clay
- pipe cleaners

Design and Build

☐ 1. **Make a model** dam that stops water. Choose your materials.

☐ 2. Design your dam. Build it in the plastic bin.

☐ 3. Test it by adding water to one side of it.

Engineering Practice

You **make a model** to show how something works.

Evaluate Your Design

4. How well did your dam hold water?

_____

_____

5. Compare your dam to others in the class. Tell which properties of matter are good for building a dam.

Measure Properties

Many properties can be measured. Scientists measure accurately. For example, you can measure temperature and weight. **Weight** is how heavy an object is.

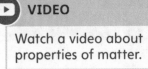
VIDEO

Watch a video about properties of matter.

measuring oranges

farmers' market

Observe Properties

You can observe the size, color, and shape of an object. Texture is another property. **Texture** is how something feels. An object may feel soft, smooth, rough, or bumpy. You can see some textures.

Crosscutting Concepts ▸ Toolbox

Patterns You can observe common shapes in nature. Look at the picture. Circle two shapes that are similar.

Visual Literacy Look at the picture. Use properties of matter to describe what you see.

Contrast Tell how the textures of the fruits and vegetables are different.

Test Properties

Some metals are magnetic. An object that can be pushed or pulled by a magnet is **magnetic.**

You can test if an object will sink or float. An object can float if it has air inside of it or if it is light and has a large surface.

INTERACTIVITY

Complete an activity on identifying properties of matter.

> **☑ Reading Check** Cause and **Effect** Underline what causes an object to float.

You may also need to test for flexibility. Matter that has **flexibility** is able to bend. If an object can scratch another object, then it is harder than that object. **Hardness** is a property that tells how hard or solid an object is compared to other objects.

objects sinking and floating

Quest Connection

Is flexibility a property of a building block? Why or why not?

Observe, Measure, Test

Some properties you can observe. Others you may need to measure or test.

Look at the images of the blocks. Which properties can you observe?

Collect Data Tell three properties of the blocks that would make them good to include in the building kit. Add your data to the chart.

Measure and Test Properties of Blocks	
Properties	**How to Measure or Test Properties**

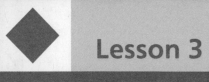

Lesson 3

Use Solids

Vocabulary

purpose

I can investigate how the properties of some solids make them useful.

2-PS1-2

Jumpstart Discovery!

Think of a solid object you use at home. Act out using the object. Do not speak. Have a partner guess what the object is. What clues did your partner use?

Which package fits the blocks?

Engineers learn about the properties of a material to know how to use it. What properties of a solid can you use to help you decide which package to use?

Procedure

☐ 1. **Observe** the size and shape of the ten blocks together.

☐ 2. Predict which container will fit all the blocks. Predict whether the blocks will change shape when moved into a container.

☐ 3. Test your prediction.

Analyze and Interpret Data

4. Which containers best fit the blocks?

_____

_____

_____

5. How do you know the blocks are solid?

_____

_____

_____

Materials

• ten building blocks

• small and large cardboard boxes

• small and large plastic bags

Science Practice

You **observe** when you look closely at things.

Uses of Solids

▶ **VIDEO**

Watch a video about using solids.

When building a house, each material has a purpose. A **purpose** is the use of an object. Wood makes the frame of the walls and roof. Bricks might be used to keep out wind, heat, or cold air. If you use brick for the roof it might fall down! You can measure the materials to decide how much you need.

☑ **Reading Check** **Cause and Effect** Underline the effect that heavy bricks could have on the roof of a house.

Everyday Solids

People use solids every day. You use a solid cup when you drink. You use a solid plate when you eat. You play with solid toys.

Solids come in many shapes and sizes. They can be different materials. They can be glass, metal, plastic, or concrete. Sometimes solids are made of more than one material.

Identify Tell what materials are used in this house. Why are the materials good for their job?

INTERACTIVITY

Complete an activity on building with solids.

Math ▸ Toolbox 🔧

Measuring Objects
Tell two ways you can measure a solid like your chair or desk. Measure one of these objects. Compare your results with a classmate.

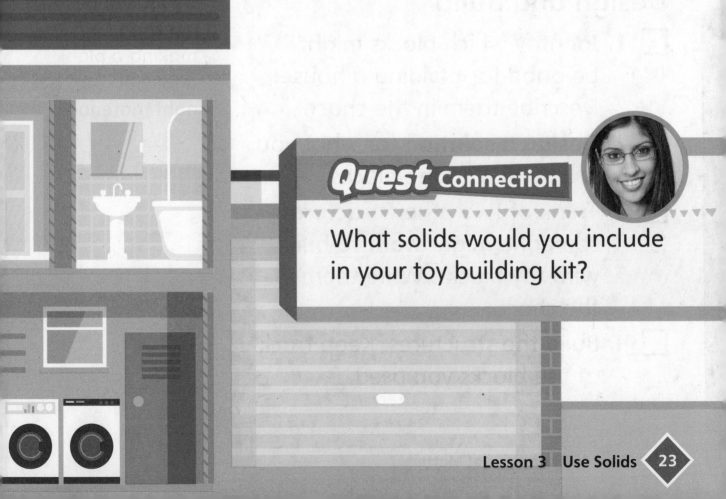

Quest Connection

What solids would you include in your toy building kit?

How do you use shapes when building?

Materials
- building blocks of different sizes and shapes

It is time to design a solution for building with shapes. We need to make a plan and choose the right materials. What materials will we use in the kit?

Design and Build

☐ **1.** Identify which blocks might be good for building a house. Describe them in the chart.

☐ **2. Design a solution** for what you will build with the blocks.

☐ **3.** Think of two other structures someone might want to build with toy blocks. Write them in the chart.

☐ **4.** Build the structures. Keep track of the blocks you used.

Item	Blocks Used
House	

Evaluate Your Design

5. How did you choose the materials for your design solution?

_____

_____

_____

6. What was the purpose of different blocks?

_____

_____

_____

_____

Lesson 4

Use Liquids and Gases

Vocabulary

state

I can investigate how the properties of some liquids and gases make them useful.

2-PS1-2

Jumpstart Discovery!

Think about gas in the form of wind, your breath, and the air around us. Draw a picture that shows different ways we use gases.

How can you make a bigger **bubble?**

Scientists study liquids and gases. How does the amount of soap compared to water affect the size of a bubble?

Procedure

☐ 1. What do you know about bubbles? Predict if more or less soap will produce a bigger bubble.

☐ 2. Make a plan to test your prediction. Use all of the materials.

☐ 3. Show your plan to your teacher. Run your test. **Collect data**.

Materials

- water
- liquid soap
- bubble wands
- graduated cylinder
- 3 plastic cups

Science Practice

Scientists **collect data** when they investigate a question.

Observations			
Test Number	Amount of water	Amount of Soap	Results
1			
2			
3			

Analyze and Interpret Data

4. Tell if your observations supported your prediction.

Shapes of Liquids and Gases

Liquids and gases do not have a shape. They take the shape of their container. Their shape changes if their container changes.

balloon animal

> ☑ **Reading Check** Cause and Effect What determines the shape of a liquid?
>
> It's contaner.

The air in your classroom is made of gases. It takes the shape of your classroom. Air inside bicycle tires is the same shape as the tires. Look at the balloon animal. It is filled with gas.

balloons

Quest Connection

Can you use liquid or gas to build a house? Why or why not?

States of Matter

You know that water can be liquid or solid. Water can also be a gas. Water that is a gas is called water vapor. You cannot see water vapor. Solid, liquid, and gas are states of matter. A **state** of matter is a form of a matter.

melting wax crayons

Identify Underline the three different states of water. Circle the name of the gas state of water.

wax crayons

Crosscutting Concepts ▸ Toolbox 🔍

Constructing Explanations Why do you think we use gas instead of liquid inside balls and tires?

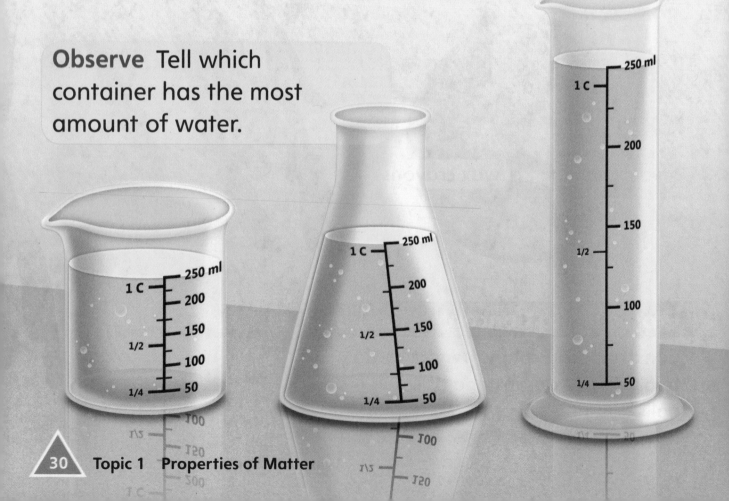

Measure Liquids

You can measure how much space a liquid or gas takes up.

You can measure liquids using containers. Pour a liquid into a container. The liquid will always take up the same amount of space. Measuring instruments make measuring liquids easy.

Identify Underline what happens to liquid when you pour it into a container.

Observe Tell which container has the most amount of water.

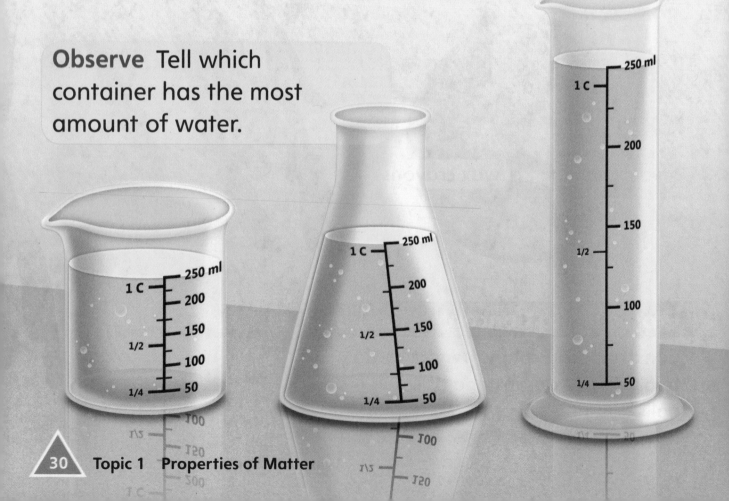

Everyday Uses of Liquids and Gases

There is liquid in the food we eat. We drink water. We also cook and wash with water. Your body is made mostly of water! Water helps you move and stay warm. Another important liquid is gasoline. We use gasoline in cars to get around. Trucks, ships, and planes use gasoline to deliver things we need.

food delivery truck

Identify Circle one way you use a liquid.

Air contains different gases. Oxygen is a gas in air. You need it to breathe. Many homes use natural gas for heating and cooking. If you see a flame in your oven or on a stove, then your home uses natural gas.

stove with natural gas

Identify Underline one way you use a gas.

Liquid and Gas Toys

You are almost ready to make the toy building kit. You have tested different solids. Now think about other states of matter. Be creative!

Explain What are some ways you could use liquids and gases in the kit?

_____

_____

_____

_____

Measure Temperature

A thermometer measures temperature. There are many different kinds of thermometers. Some are digital. Some use a liquid called alcohol inside the thermometer. As the temperature rises, alcohol expands, or gets bigger. The alcohol rises inside the thermometer as the temperature rises.

Read the temperature on each thermometer. Write the temperatures in the boxes.

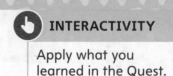

INTERACTIVITY

Apply what you learned in the Quest.

Toy Building Kit

Why do we use different materials for a toy kit?

Phenomenon Look back at your chart. Choose the best materials for the kit to make model buildings.

Show What You Found

Identify which materials go into the kit. You can make a list of the objects. You can also draw them. Try making the kit. Remember to include any packing materials. What are some similarities of the objects in the kit? What are some differences? What properties of objects make them good for building?

Toy Engineer

Toy engineers make toys. They often work on a team. It is their job to make a toy the best it can be. They test toys to make sure they are safe. They make toys easier to build. They pick the best materials to use for a type of toy. Some use computers to design or test toys. Others work in the toy factory.

Toy engineers pay attention to materials. They observe properties of the materials to make the toy better.

Why is this an important job?

_____

_____

_____

_____

_____

_____

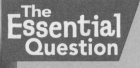

The Essential Question

How can different materials be used?

Show What You Learned

Tell a partner how you can use a solid, a liquid, and a gas for certain jobs.

1. **What are three states of matter?**

    1. _____

    _____

    2. _____

    _____

    3. _____

    _____

2. **How would you describe the properties of this ball?**

    a. large, smooth, blue
    b. small, bumpy, green
    c. large, bumpy, orange
    d. small, soft, orange

3. What material would you use for each job?
Draw a line from the job to the material.

   a. Fill a swimming pool.   air

   b. Build a house.   ice cube

   c. Fill a birthday balloon.   water

   d. Cool a glass of lemonade.   wood

4. Look at the picture. Circle one example of
a liquid. Put an X on a gas. Draw a box
around a solid.

5. Describe the shape of a solid, a liquid, and
a gas.

Read this scenario and answer questions 1–4.

A class is having a party at school! They have balloons of all colors. The students play games. The teacher puts water in a big tub. She puts toys in it to play with. A toy yellow duck is on top of the water. A toy green frog is at the bottom of the water.

Max makes lemonade for the party. He pours water into a glass. Then he adds a lemon slice. The students also have good things to eat.

1. Rita looks at the toys in the tub of water. Which of the following is a property of the toy duck in the tub?
   a. It is liquid.
   b. It floats.
   c. It is green.
   d. It sinks.

2. The students play with the balloons. One balloon pops. Write what happens to the gas inside the balloon.

_____

_____

_____

_____

_____

3. Which of the following changes shape when Max makes the lemonade?

   a. glass

   b. lemon

   c. water

   d. Max

4. Sarah observes two of the toys. One feels soft and smooth. The other feels rough and bumpy.

Circle the word that correctly completes the sentence.

size   color   texture   weight

She observes the _____ of the toys.

What makes something sink or float?

Phenomenon Boat engineers collect data about if materials sink or float before they build a boat. How can you collect data to tell which objects sink or float?

Materials

- bin
- water

Suggested Materials

- paperclips
- corks
- erasers
- craft sticks
- foil sheets
- small balloons
- clay

Procedure

☐ **1.** Choose and observe four objects. Predict if each one will sink or float.

☐ **2.** Make a plan to test each object. Show your plan to your teacher.

☐ **3.** Run your test. **Collect data** in the table.

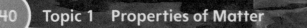

Observations

Object	Observed Properties	Sink or Float?

Analyze and Interpret Data

4. **Explain** Why do some objects float and why do some objects sink?

_____

- -

_____

5. **CCC Patterns** Decide if one of the objects you did not test will sink or float. How do you know whether it will sink or float?

_____

- -

_____

_____

_____

Changing Matter

Next Generation Science Standards

2-PS1-1 Plan and conduct an investigation to describe and classify different kinds of materials by their observable properties.

2-PS1-3 Make observations to construct an evidence-based account of how an object made of a small set of pieces can be disassembled and made into a new object.

2-PS1-4 Construct an argument with evidence that some changes caused by heating or cooling can be reversed and some cannot.

Go online to access
your digital course.

▶ VIDEO

📖 eTEXT

👆 INTERACTIVITY

▶ SCIENCE SONG

🎮 GAME

☑ ASSESSMENT

The Essential Question

How do you change materials?

Show What You Know

Look at the photo. Tell how the ice is changing.

Building Bridges

What are the best materials
to use in building a bridge?

Phenomenon Hi! My name is Ms. Kuan.
I am an engineer. I am working at a
construction site. We are building some tall
buildings. We need to build a bridge. It will
connect different areas of the site.

The bridge needs to be strong. It will carry
people and trucks. The bridge will be used
in summer and winter. Sometimes it will
be used in high winds. Help me find
the best materials we should use to
build the best bridge for this job.
The path shows the Quest activities
you will complete as you work
through the topic. Check off your
progress each time you complete an
activity with a QUEST CHECK ✓ OFF .

Quest Check-In

Lesson 1 ◼ ◯

Use what you
learned to identify
changes to matter.

Next Generation Science Standards

2-PS1-3 Make observations to construct an evidence-based account of how an object
made of a smawll set of pieces can be disassembled and made into a new object.

2-PS1-4 Construct an argument with evidence that some changes caused by heating
or cooling can be reversed and some cannot.

VIDEO

Watch a video about building bridges.

Quest Check-In 2

Lesson 2 ●

Use what you learned to tell how matter is changed by heating and cooling.

Quest Check-In Lab 3

Lesson 3 ◆

Use what you learned to make one large object from many smaller objects.

Quest Findings

Complete the Quest! Write a letter describing the best materials to use to build a bridge.

How can you use all of the materials?

Engineers use a list of materials to build a structure. What can you build that uses all of the materials?

Design a Solution

☐ **1.** Use all of the materials to build a structure. Make a plan.

☐ **2.** Build your structure.

☐ **3.** Trade objects with another group. **Make observations.**

Evaluate Designs

4. **Explain** Tell how your structure was alike and different from the others.

5. **Explain** Tell how other groups used the same materials to build a different structure.

Materials

- cardboard tubes
- pieces of cardboard
- craft sticks
- toothpicks
- glue
- tape
- paper clips
- scissors

⚠ **Be careful using scissors.**

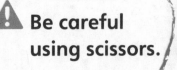
Engineering Practice

You make observations to help collect evidence and make explanations.

Sequence

Scientists need to follow steps in a **sequence** to do a job. Sequence means to put steps in order.

GAME

Practice what you learn with the Mini Games.

A Cool Snack

Here is a recipe to make frozen juice pops. First, get some fruit. Next, have an adult cut the fruit into small pieces. Then, put the fruit pieces into the blender. Watch as the blender turns the fruit into juice. Pour the juice into an ice cube tray. Finally, put the ice cube tray into the freezer. After 4-6 hours, you will have frozen juice pops.

☑ **Reading Check**   **Sequence** Underline the sentence with the word *First*. Draw a circle around something that happens next. Draw a square around the thing that happens last.

Why is it important to follow a sequence in a recipe?

_____

Lesson 1

Observe Changes in Matter

Vocabulary

matter

I can explore different ways matter can change.

2-PS1-1

Jumpstart Discovery!

Hold a piece of paper. Change the paper. Can you undo the change?

How can you *change* objects?

Scientists observe how objects can be changed. How many ways can you change something?

Materials

- clay
- 3 to 5 drops of food coloring
- plastic gloves

Procedure

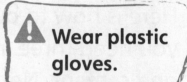

⚠ **Wear plastic gloves.**

☐ 1. Use the materials. Make a plan to make at least three changes.

☐ 2. Show your teacher your plan.

☐ 3. Follow your plan. Make observations.

Science Practice

You **construct explanations** when you use evidence from your observations.

Analyze and Interpret Data

4. **Explain** Tell if you made changes that could be undone. What were they?

5. **Explain** Tell if you made changes that could not be undone. What were they?

Matter Can Change

Think about the sidewalk at school. The sidewalk is made of matter. **Matter** is anything that takes up space. The sidewalk is a solid, but it is made up of three types of matter including liquid water.

Here is how to build a sidewalk. First, you need three ingredients: water, sand, and cement. Next, mix the sand and cement together. Then, slowly add the water until the mixture is almost too hard to stir. Now, these ingredients are called concrete. Finally, your concrete is ready to pour to make your sidewalk.

☑ **Reading Check** **Sequence**
Underline the first thing you need to do to make a sidewalk.

Quest Connection

Tell how the materials you use to build a bridge will decide what properties it has.

You Can Change Matter

Sometimes you can change the features of matter. You can change solid matter by cutting, bending, and folding it. You can change matter by tearing, taking it apart, and breaking it. You take a ball of clay. You make an animal shape. You change the features of the clay. You can change the clay back to its original shape.

Large machines are used to mix and pour concrete to make a sidewalk.

▶ INTERACTIVITY

Show how you can change matter.

Matter Changes in Many Ways

You can make orange juice from fresh oranges. You change the solid fruit into a liquid. You cannot change the orange juice back into oranges though! Matter does not always change in the exact same way. Sometimes you can undo the change you made. Sometimes you cannot.

You make a change in matter. The object you changed looks different from its original shape or form. A flat piece of paper can be used for writing or coloring. If you make a paper animal, the paper looks completely different. The paper animal also has a different purpose. You play with the animal, you don't write on it.

Matter Can Change

Look at the photos. Each photo shows how matter can change. Sometimes you can change the matter back to what it used to be. Sometimes you cannot.

Classify Circle the changes you can undo. Put an X on the changes you cannot undo.

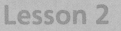

Temperature and Matter

Vocabulary

property

reversible

I can explain whether a change caused by heating or cooling matter is reversible.

I can explain whether a change caused by heating or cooling matter is not reversible.

2-PS1-4

Jumpstart Discovery!

What is happening to the crayons? Act it out.

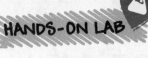
How does heating and cooling change matter?

Scientists learn how matter changes when it is heated or cooled. What observations can you make about the claim that heating or cooling changes matter?

Procedure

☐ 1. Make a plan to add heat to the crayon and to chill the crayon.

☐ 2. Show your plan to your teacher before you start.

☐ 3. Record your results.

Analyze and Interpret Data

4. **Explain** Tell if you could make the crayon look exactly the way it did when you started.

Materials

- crayons
- freezer
- heat source
- thermometer
- ice cube trays
- metal spoon
- oven mitt

Science Practice

You use evidence to support a claim.

⚠ **Do not touch heat source.**

⚠ **Wear gloves when handling hot or cold objects.**

Temperature

You can observe the properties of matter. A **property** is something about an object you can observe with your senses. Temperature is a property of matter. How hot or cold is it outside? You can measure this property of matter with a thermometer. A thermometer is a tool that measures how hot or cold it is.

Monday	Tuesday	Wednesday	Thursday	Friday
Sunshine	Rain	Clouds	Sunny	Sunny
26 °C (80 °F)	20 °C (68 °F)	22 °C (72 °F)	25 °C (77 °F)	28 °C (83 °F)

Monday	Tuesday	Wednesday	Thursday	Friday

VIDEO

Watch a video about heating and cooling.

Heating and Cooling

The place where polar bears live has both liquid water and solid ice. This place is called the Arctic. The temperatures in the Arctic are very cold. Cold can change matter. In the winter the liquid water freezes. It turns to solid ice. Some of the ice stays in its solid shape year round.

In the summer the temperatures in the Arctic are warm. Warmth can also change matter. Some of the solid ice that formed in the winter melts. It turns to liquid water. These changes caused by heating and cooling happen over and over again, year after year.

Quest Connection

Tell how temperature changes can help you decide what materials to use to build your bridge.

Reversible or Not

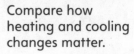
INTERACTIVITY

Compare how heating and cooling changes matter.

Some changes made by heating and cooling can be **reversible**. They can be changed back to the way they were.

Some changes made by heating and cooling cannot be changed. They can never be changed back to the way they were.

Identify Which change can be reversed? Circle it.

Which change cannot be reversed? Put an X on it.

How does temperature change matter over time?

Think about different materials that could be used for a bridge. Some bridges are made of rope. Others might use steel coils or concrete columns. How might the temperature affect each of these materials?

Steel coil

Look at the chart. The chart shows materials that might be good to use to build a bridge. Some materials are a good choice for both cold and warm weather.

Surfaces for Bridges	Properties in Warm Weather	Properties in Cold Weather	Best in All Kinds of Weather
Rope	strong, may be slippery when wet	strong, but could be dangerous in icy weather	
Concrete	strong, and good in warm weather	strong, and good in cold weather	
Wood	strong, may be slippery when wet	strong, but could be dangerous in icy weather	

Identify Which surface has the best properties for both warm and cold weather? Put an X in that row. Tell why.

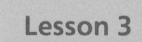
Matter Within Objects

▶ VIDEO

Watch a video that shows smaller objects being used to build larger objects.

Vocabulary

assemble

I can explain that objects can be built using smaller materials.

I can explain that objects are built using materials that have certain properties.

2-PS1-3

Jumpstart Discovery!

Look at the roller coaster. What is it made of? Think of one word to describe the roller coaster. Tell a partner!

What can you build?

Look at the list of materials. How can you use these objects to build something?

Design a Solution

☐ 1. Think of a problem you want to solve. Choose materials. **Design a Solution.**

☐ 2. Show your plan to your teacher.

☐ 3. Build your solution.

☐ 4. Tell another group how your design works.

Evaluate Your Design

5. Did your solution solve the problem you identified? Why or why not?

_____

_____

_____

_____

6. How can you change your design to make it better?

_____

_____

_____

_____

_____

Suggested Materials

- building blocks
- cardboard
- toothpicks
- craft sticks
- pipe cleaners
- glue
- tape
- clothes pins
- clay
- safety scissors

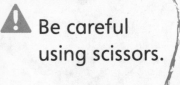 Be careful using scissors.

Engineering Practice

You **design a solution** when you plan to build something to solve a problem.

Objects Can Be Assembled from Other Objects

🖱 **INTERACTIVITY**

Learn to take something apart to make something new.

A small model of a real plane has many parts. When you put the parts together, you assemble them to make your model plane. **Assemble** means to put together. There is a sequence you have to follow in order to correctly put something together. Look at the pictures. They are not in the correct order. Show how you can you put a model plane together.

Visual Literacy

Sequence Number the steps to show how you would put the plane together in the proper sequence.

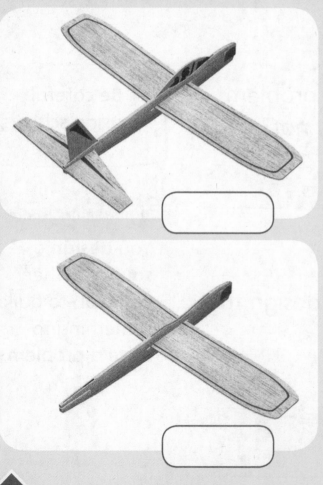

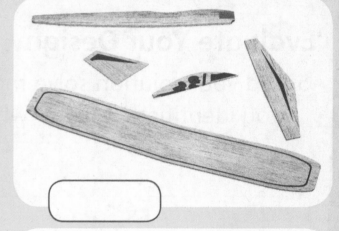

Choose one of the objects shown. Draw a large object made up of many of the small objects. Write a caption for your drawing. Label one of the small objects. Then explain what the purpose was of the object you drew.

Quest Connection

Tell how you can use many small objects to make a large object, such as a bridge.

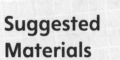
What materials make a bridge strong?

Bridges are used for different purposes in different places. What materials will you use to make your bridge strong?

Suggested Materials

- two desks
- string
- craft sticks
- cardboard
- plastic cups
- straws
- pipe cleaners
- glue

Design and Build

☐ 1. **Design a solution.** You need a strong bridge to cross the space between two desks.

☐ 2. Choose materials to build your bridge.

☐ 3. Show your plan to your teacher.

☐ 4. Build your bridge. Record each material you used.

☐ 5. Test how strong your bridge is by putting blocks on it.

Engineering Practice

Engineers **design a solution** to a problem by making a plan and choosing the right materials.

Evaluate Your Design

6. **Evaluate** Tell which materials worked best for your bridge. Explain.

Compare Numbers

Scientists use the Celsius scale to measure temperature.

When water freezes, it measures 0 °Celsius (C). It can also be measured as 32 °Fahrenheit (F). The ° symbol means *degrees*.

Look at the thermometers. To tell the temperature you look at the top of the red line and read the numbers on either side of it.

Circle the summer temperature. Put an X on the winter temperature. Write these two temperatures below. How do these numbers compare?

uEngineer It! Improve STEM

Improve a Sipping Cup!

INTERACTIVITY

Go online to learn more about how certain materials are used for specific purposes.

Phenomenon Your baby sister uses a sipping cup to drink her milk. She brings it to her mouth. It leaks all over her. The cup is not supposed to leak. Something is wrong with this cup! Can you tell what the problem is by looking at the picture? Think about how you can stop the cup from leaking.

Improve It

Think about the materials you would need to build a new sipping cup for your sister that doesn't leak. What are the parts of the cup that you will need to assemble a new cup? What will your design be to solve this problem?

- ☐ Draw a design of a sipping cup.
- ☐ Label the materials used in each part of the cup.
- ☐ Share your design. Compare it to another design.

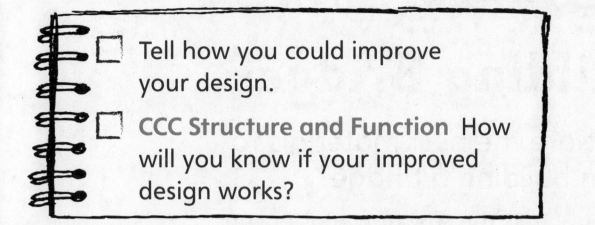

- [ ] Tell how you could improve your design.

- [ ] **CCC Structure and Function** How will you know if your improved design works?

INTERACTIVITY

Apply your Quest learnings to a new scenario.

Building Bridges

What are the best materials to use in building a bridge?

Phenomenon You saw how matter can change. You saw how hot weather and cold weather could change matter. You built a model bridge. You chose materials to make it strong.

Show What You Found

Write a letter to Ms. Kuan. Explain to her which materials you think she can use to build her bridge. You can make a list of the materials. You can also draw them. Tell Ms. Kuan why you think these materials are the best to use to build a strong bridge in warm and cold weather.

QUEST CHECK ✓ OFF

Structural Engineer

Structural engineers design things you use every day. They design buildings, bridges, tunnels, and homes. They often work together as a team. It is their job to make sure that what they build is safe and strong. They also need to make sure they use the right materials to get the job done. Structural engineers work at construction sites and many other places.

Structural engineers pay attention to materials used to build things. They observe a material's properties to make sure the project does what it needs to do.

Tell why is this an important job.

The Essential Question How do you change materials?

Show What You Learned
Tell a partner how you can change ice into water.

1. Which of the following changes of matter can you undo?
   a. Apples changed into apple juice
   b. Crackers broken into pieces
   c. Paper torn into pieces
   d. Paper folded to make an airplane

2. Which of the following changes of matter were made by heating?
   a. Corn kernels into popcorn
   b. Juice into juice pops
   c. Water into ice cubes
   d. Oranges into orange juice

3. You measure the temperature every day for a week. What can this help you decide?
   a. What to eat for breakfast
   b. What lunch to take to school
   c. What to wear outside to play
   d. What time to catch the bus

4. Which of these is an example of a reversible change?

    a. Clay being rolled into a ball

    b. Paper being torn

    c. A cut up banana

    d. A sliced loaf of bread

5. Look at the pictures of the sandwich. What is the correct sequence to make the sandwich?

    a. ABCD

    b. ADCB

    c. BCDA

    d. DBCA

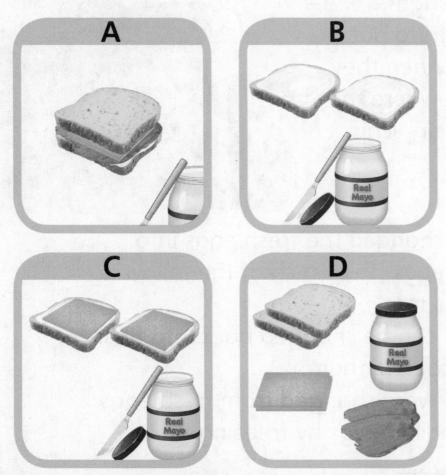

Read and answer questions 1–4.

Christopher and his family decided to go on a picnic. They prepared food to eat for their lunch. They put fresh eggs in boiling water to make hard boiled eggs. They squeezed lemons and added honey and water to make lemonade. They cut up pieces of cheese and brought a box of crackers for a snack. They poured fresh orange juice into molds and put them in the freezer to make juice pops. Then they brought bread, turkey, sliced cheese, and mustard to make sandwiches. Finally, they brought a folded tablecloth to put on the ground when they got to the park where they were having their picnic.

1. Christopher changed the fresh eggs into hard boiled eggs. Tell which of the following statements is true.

   a. The eggs can be changed back into fresh eggs by cooling them.

   b. The eggs were changed from fresh eggs to hard boiled eggs by freezing them.

c. The eggs cannot be changed back into fresh eggs after they have been boiled.

d. The eggs cannot be changed from fresh eggs into hard boiled eggs by boiling them.

2. Which of the following used cooling as a way to change matter?

a. lemons, honey and water into lemonade

b. orange juice into juice pops

c. fresh eggs into hard boiled eggs

d. cutting up cheese for a snack

3. Which of the following can be changed back to its original shape?

a. a folded tablecloth

b. cut up pieces of cheese

c. lemonade from lemons, honey, and water

d. broken crackers

4. Tell how to use the cheese, turkey, bread, and mustard to make a sandwich. Use the words "first," "next," and "last."

_____

_____

_____

_____

_____

_____

How can you make something new?

Materials

• blocks of different sizes and colors

Phenomenon Engineers use the objects they have to make something new. They think about what the object must do. They find the parts they need. They assemble the parts into something new.

Engineering Practice

Engineers make observations to help collect evidence and make explanations.

Design Solutions

☐ **1.** Look at the blocks. Identify a problem you want to solve. Build a structure with all the blocks to solve the problem.

☐ **2.** Draw your structure.

☐ **3.** Identify a second problem you want to solve. Build a new structure with all the same blocks to solve the second problem.

☐ **4.** CCC Energy and Matter Draw your new structure.

Analyze and Interpret Data

☐ **5. Explain** how each structure solved a problem.

_____

- -

_____

- -

_____

☐ **6. Explain** how you used the same materials
    to solve two problems.

_____

- -

_____

- -

_____

Earth's Water and Land

Next Generation Science Standards

2-ESS2-1 Compare multiple solutions designed to slow or prevent wind or water from changing the shape of the land.

2-ESS2-2 Develop a model to represent the shapes and kinds of land and bodies of water in an area.

2-ESS2-3 Obtain information to identify where water is found on Earth and that it can be solid or liquid.

K-2-ETS1-3 Analyze data from tests of two objects designed to solve the same problem to compare the strengths and weaknesses of how each performs.

Go online to access
your digital course.

▶ VIDEO

📖 eTEXT

👆 INTERACTIVITY

▶ SCIENCE SONG

🎮 GAME

☑ ASSESSMENT

The Essential Question

How can you describe land and water on Earth?

Show What You Know

Put an **X** on one landform in the picture. Tell a partner the name of the landform.

Map Your Hike!

How can we draw a map?

Phenomenon I am Ms. Imani. I am a map maker, and I need your help. I am making a map for hikers going on a scavenger hunt. To complete the hunt, hikers must take pictures of land and water. Hikers must find two landforms. Hikers must find two bodies of water. The hunt ends at a swimming hole where there will be a picnic.

Help me map a good hiking trail! As you read, look for different landforms and bodies of water. You will also learn how to make a map.

The path shows the Quest activities you will complete as you work through the topic. Check off your progress each time you complete an activity with a QUEST CHECK ✓ OFF .

Quest Check-In Lab 1

Lesson 1 ■
Use what you learned to model landforms.

2-ESS2-1 Compare multiple solutions designed to slow or prevent wind or water from changing the shape of the land. **2-ESS2-2** Develop a model to represent the shapes and kinds of land and bodies of water in an area. [Assessment Boundary: **2-ESS2-3** Obtain information to identify where water is found on and that it can be solid or liquid.

VIDEO

Watch a video about a map maker.

Quest Check-In 2

○ **Lesson 2** ●

Use what you learned to describe bodies of water.

Quest Check-In Lab 3

○ **Lesson 3** ◆

Use what you learned to measure distance on a map.

Quest Findings

○ Complete the Quest! Make a map of a trail that will take hikers to a mountain, a stream, a rocky shore, and a swimming hole!

What covers most of the surface of Earth?

How can you find out whether water or land covers more of the surface of Earth?

Materials

- Land and Water Sheet
- blue and green counting cubes

Procedure

☐ **1.** Use the map and materials to find information and see if there is more water or land on Earth.

☐ **2.** Collect information and record it.

Science Practice

You **get information** to answer a scientific question.

Measurement	Land (green)	Water (blue)
Number of Counting Cubes		

Analyze and Interpret Data

3. Draw Conclusions Does the map show more water or more land? How do you know?

_____

_____

_____

_____

Picture Clues

Looking at pictures before and after you read can help you understand the text.

Read the text and look at the picture.

Climbing Denali

Would you like to climb the highest mountain in North America? You would need to travel to Alaska. You would climb a mountain called Denali. Its peak soars up to 6,190 meters high! Climbing the mountain is hard. Many people climb to the top each year. The best time to climb Denali is in late May and June. The trip takes between 17 to 21 days!

✅ **Reading Check** **Picture Clues** What is one thing you can see in the photo that is not in the text? Tell a partner what you see.

Lesson 1

Describe Earth's Surface

Vocabulary

landform

slope

plains

plateau

canyon

I can identify different landforms on Earth's surface.

2-ESS2-2, 2-ESS2-3

Jumpstart Discovery!

Close your eyes. Point to a place on a map or globe. Is it land or water? How do you know? Is the water solid or liquid? How do you know?

How can you make a map of a special place?

How would you tell a friend how to get to one of your favorite places?

Materials

• drawing materials

Science Practice

You **use models** to learn more about real-life places.

Procedure

☐ 1. Think of a place you like to go.

☐ 2. Draw and label a map of the place. Write the name of the place on your map.

Analyze and Interpret Data

3. **Communicate** What did you learn about making a map?

_____

_____

_____

The Surface of Earth

Most maps are flat. The surface of Earth is not flat. The surface of Earth has many different landforms. A **landform** is a feature made of rock and dirt. Landforms are different sizes and shapes.

Mountains

The highest landforms are mountains. Mountains are large landforms that can be very high. Some mountains are so high that the snow on top of them never melts. Most mountains have pointed tops, or peaks. Mountains have steep slopes. A **slope** is an area that slants up. Steep slopes make mountains very hard to climb.

INTERACTIVITY

Go online to learn about different landforms.

Crosscutting Concepts ▸ Toolbox

Stability and Change
The surface of Earth is always changing. Some changes, like volcanoes and earthquakes, are very fast. Wind and water can cause fast changes or slow changes.

☑ **Reading Check** Picture Clues
Draw an **X** on the slope of the mountain.

Quest Connection

Would it be easier to hike over a mountain or over a hill? Tell one reason why.

Hills and Plains

A hill is a landform that is higher than the land around it. They are not as high as mountains. Snow melts off them in warmer weather.

A low area between mountains or hills is called a valley. There are many different types of valleys.

Plains are flat areas that are often in valleys. Plains are very important landforms because they often have very rich soil. Soil is loose material that plants can grow in. Soil contains living things like bacteria, small animals, and insects. Soil contains nonliving things like minerals, bits of rocks, water, and air. Because they are flat, many plains are used for farming.

valleys

plains

mountains and hills

Plateaus and Canyons

Plateaus are raised parts of Earth's surface that are flat on top.

Sometimes plateaus have canyons below. **Canyons** are deep valleys. The valleys in the canyons have steep walls. Many canyons are formed by rivers. Rivers carry dirt and rock away. Over time, the canyon forms.

Explain Tell a partner how canyons are formed.

Literacy ▸ Toolbox

Picture Clues Look at the pictures. Why would it be difficult to hike from the bottom of a canyon to the top of a plateau?

plateaus and canyons

Landforms on the Ocean Floor

The ocean floor has landforms, too. Many of the landforms on the ocean floor are much bigger than the landforms on land.

Many people think Mount Everest in Asia is the highest mountain on Earth. Mauna Kea in Hawaii is much higher. The base of Mauna Kea is on the ocean floor, making it the tallest mountain in the world.

Challenger Deep is the deepest canyon in the ocean. It is much deeper than Mount Everest is high!

Explain Underline words that explain why Mauna Kea is the tallest mountain in the world.

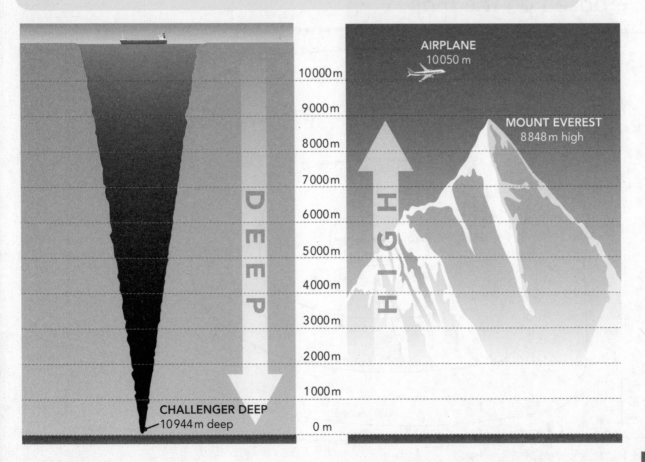

AIRPLANE
10050 m

10000 m

9000 m

MOUNT EVEREST
8848 m high

8000 m

7000 m

D
E
E
P

6000 m

H
I
G
H

5000 m

4000 m

3000 m

2000 m

1000 m

CHALLENGER DEEP
10944 m deep

0 m

How can you model landforms?

Most maps are flat. Map makers use 3-D models to study how tall a landform might be. How can you model a landform?

Materials
- modeling clay in several colors

Procedure

☐ **1.** Look at the map.

☐ **2.** Use the materials to build a model based on the map.

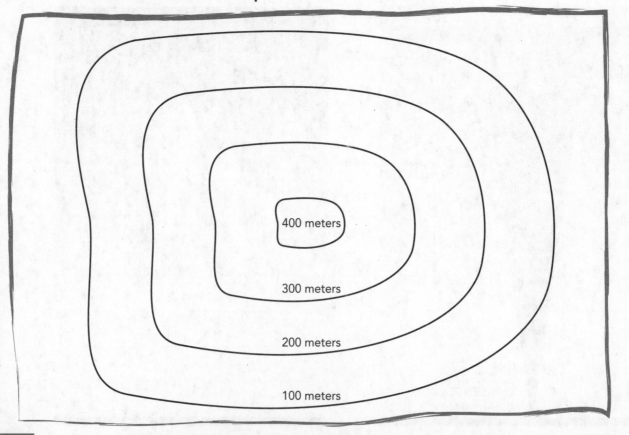

400 meters

300 meters

200 meters

100 meters

Analyze and Interpret Data

3. **Identify** What is the highest location on your model of the map? How high is that location?

_____

_____

_____

_____

4. **Use Models** According to the model, would it be easier to hike around the hill or over it? Why?

_____

_____

_____

_____

Lesson 2

Water on Earth

▶ **VIDEO**

Watch a video about different bodies of water.

Vocabulary

fresh water

glacier

I can identify different bodies of water.

I can tell whether a body of water is solid or liquid.

2-ESS2-2, 2-ESS2-3

Jumpstart Discovery!

Pretend you are an ice cube, a mountain stream, or an ocean. Act it out! Let a partner guess what you are.

uInvestigate Lab

Where is the best place to cross the water?

How can you use a map to tell where you can cross water?

Materials
• River and Stream Sheet

Science Practice

You **use a model** to explore solutions.

Procedure

☐ **1.** Look at the River and Stream Sheet. Decide where the best places for crossing the river are located.

☐ **2.** Write your observations in the table.

Point	How wide?	How can I cross it?
1		
2		
3		

Analyze and Interpret Data

3. Evaluate Where is it easiest to cross the river if you are walking? Why?

_____

_____

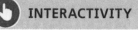

INTERACTIVITY

Go online to learn more about solid and liquid bodies of water on Earth.

The Ocean

Water covers almost three-fourths of the surface of Earth. Most of Earth's water is found in the ocean. There is one very large ocean with several named basins. Many people think the ocean and seas are the same. Seas have land around most sides.

Salty ocean water gets its salt from the rivers that flow into it from all over the surface of Earth.

Rivers and Streams

Earth also has fresh water. You can find fresh water in glaciers, streams, rivers, lakes, and ponds. **Fresh water** is water that has very little salt. Most animals, plants, and humans depend on fresh water to live.

Streams are bodies of flowing water. Depending on their size and other features, they are given different names like rivers and creeks.

river

ocean

Glaciers

Glaciers are very large bodies of flowing ice. They move downhill very slowly. They are solid water. Many glaciers start out as snow at the tops of mountains. Glaciers form when snow stays in one place long enough to form ice. Glaciers pick up rocks and dirt as they move and bring them to different places.

glacier

Identify Write two bodies of liquid water. Write one body of solid water.

_____

_____

_____

_____

_____

☑ **Reading Check** **Picture Clues** Put an **X** on a photo of a river. How do you know?

_____

_____

_____

_____

Lakes and Ponds

Some streams and rivers feed into lakes. Most lakes have fresh water. There are also some salt water lakes. Lakes are very large bodies of water that have land around them on all sides, except where streams flow into and out of them. They are usually deeper than rivers. You can see waves when the wind blows on the water. Some lakes are called ponds.

Math ▸ Toolbox

Fractions Imagine that the surface of Earth is a pie. You can cut the pie into four equal pieces. Almost three of the four pieces of pie would be ocean!

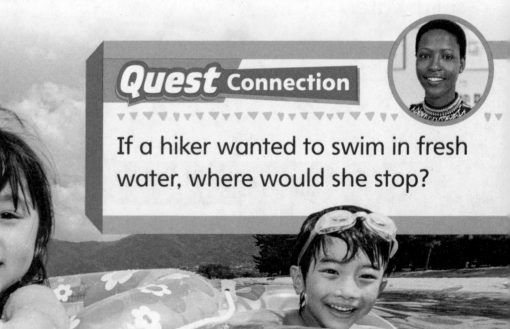

Quest Connection

If a hiker wanted to swim in fresh water, where would she stop?

Describe Earth's Water

Look at the pictures. Answer the questions.

river   lake   glacier

1. Which bodies of water can you hike across?

_____

_____

2. Where would a hiker need a bridge to
   cross the water?

_____

_____

3. Which bodies of water would a hiker walk beside?

_____

_____

4. Which body of water could you swim across?

_____

_____

uEngineer It! — Improve — STEM

K-2-ETS1-3, SEP.2, SEP.6

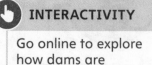

INTERACTIVITY

Go online to explore how dams are repaired.

Improve a Dam!

Phenomenon Animals and people build dams to hold back the water in rivers and streams. Look at the dam in the picture. How can you make it better?

Improve It

Improve this dam. It must stop the water.
It also needs to let some of the water through.

- ☐ Draw a plan for making the dam better. Share your drawing with a partner.

- ☐ Label the materials you use.

- ☐ Tell how each material stops the water from flowing.

Observations

☐ Write how your plan will make
the dam better.

_____

- - - - - - - - - - - - - - - -

_____

- - - - - - - - - - - - - - - -

_____

☐ What do you think happens to the
environment downstream when the
flow of water is blocked?

_____

- - - - - - - - - - - - - - - -

_____

- - - - - - - - - - - - - - - -

_____

Map Land and Water

▶ **VIDEO**

Watch a video about different types of maps.

Vocabulary

model
key
scale

I can use maps to show where land and water are on Earth.

2-ESS2-2

Jumpstart Discovery!

How would you hike across water? How would you hike across different landforms? Act it out!

Why do map makers
use different maps?

What can people learn from different kinds of maps?

Materials
- Aerial and Street Map Sheet

Procedure

☐ **1.** Look at the different maps. They show the same location.

☐ **2.** Identify what is different about each map.

☐ **3.** Record your observations in the chart.

Science Practice

You **use models** to study what something is like in real life.

Street Map	Aerial Map	Observations

Analyze and Interpret Data

4. Evaluate Tell which map you would choose to show a friend how to get to one of the locations.

INTERACTIVITY

Go online to learn more about making maps.

Understand a Map

A map is a model. A **model** is a copy of something. There can be many different maps for the same area. One map of a museum might show you where it is in town. Another map of the same museum might show you where to go for a snack.

Maps need a **key**. A key explains what pictures or signs on the map mean. Look at this map of a museum. Can you use the key to find a place to eat?

Many maps also have a scale. Maps are much smaller than the real places. A **scale** is a way to compare the distance between two objects on the map and those same objects in real life.

i	Information
	Elevator
	Restroom
	Water
	Coats
	Audio
	Gift shop
	Food
	Escalator

KEY

Visual Literacy

Choose two places. Use the scale to write how far away one place is from the other.

_____

_____

_____

_____

Crosscutting Concepts ▸ Toolbox

Scale, Proportion, and Quantity Think of another way you can compare the sizes of two objects without using a measuring tool. Write or draw your idea.

Quest Connection

What is one thing your hiking map will show that the museum map does not show?

0 1 2 3 4 5
Scale in Meters

SCALE

How far is it from here to there?

How can you measure distance on a map?

Materials
- Street Map Sheet
- ruler

Procedure

Science Practice

You **use models** to draw objects to scale.

☐ **1.** Look at the map. Measure the distance between two places on the map. Repeat this step two more times with different locations.

☐ **2.** Record your data in the chart.

Point A	Point B	Distance

Analyze and Interpret Data

3. Explain Tell how you found the distance between Point A and Point B on the map.

4. Apply Concepts Tell if there is a shorter way to get from one point to another on the map. Give directions.

Measure Distance

Football fields are usually measured in yards. You can use the scale to guess the size of this football field in meters.

Measure The length of a football field can be measured in meters.

```
0      10     20
├───┼───┼───┤
    meters
```

About how many meters long is this football field?

About how wide is it?

Map Your Hike!

How can we make a map?

Phenomenon It's time to make your map. How can you draw a map? Use a separate sheet of paper. Remember, the map is for a scavenger hunt. Hikers will reach a swimming hole where they will have a picnic!

The hiker must see two landforms and two bodies of water while following your map. Then the hiker must end up at the swimming hole. Look through the pages. They can give you ideas of what to include.

Include a key and scale on your map.

QUEST CHECK ✓ OFF

Map Maker

Map makers can draw maps by hand. They can also use computers. Once the map is made, the map can be printed on paper.

Before a map maker gets to work, she asks questions. She asks, "Why do you need this map? What do you need the map to show?" Then the map maker gets to work. She wants the map to be helpful to the people who use it.

If you were a map maker, what map would you would like to draw? Why?

The Essential Question

How can you describe land and water on Earth?

Show What You Learned
Tell a partner what you learned about landforms and bodies of water.

1. How are landforms alike?
   a. All landforms have steep slopes.
   b. All landforms are difficult to climb.
   c. All landforms are the same shape and size.
   d. All landforms are made of rock and dirt.

2. What features do the pictures show?

_____ _____ _____

_____ _____ _____

3. How are rivers and glaciers alike? How are they different?

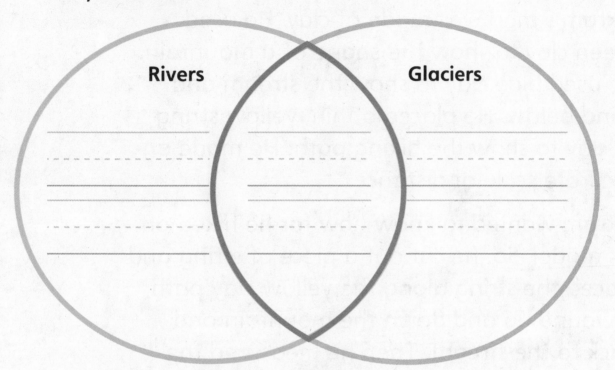

Rivers

Glaciers

4. A map scale shows 1 centimeter = 10 kilometers. If two towns are 3 centimeters apart on the map, how far away are they?

5. How can a map key help a hiker?

Read the text and answer the questions.

Bikram's map was made of clay. He used green clay to show the shape of a mountain. He used blue clay to show the stream and pond below. He placed a thin, yellow string of clay to show the hiking path. He made an accurate scale of distance.

Bikram wanted to know how far he hiked on his model. So, he cut out a piece of string and placed the string along the yellow clay path. It wound up and down the mountain and back to the stream. Then he measured the string and compared it to the scale. He had hiked five kilometers!

1. How did Bikram show the difference between land and water in his model?
   a. The land was all blue clay, and the water was all green clay.
   b. The mountain was blue clay, and the water was yellow clay.
   c. The water was blue clay, and the stream was a string of yellow clay.
   d. The water was all blue clay, and the land was all green clay.

2. How did Bikram figure out how long the hike was?

_____

- -

_____

3. Why was a string used instead of a ruler to measure the length of the hike?
   a. A string is shorter than the hike.
   b. The ruler did not have kilometer markings.
   c. A string can bend and curve, but a ruler cannot.
   d. The string was available, and the ruler was not.

4. How could Bikram change the map to make his hike harder?

_____

- -

_____

5. Circle all the places that Bikram's map shows.

mountain	plateau	river
glacier	stream	canyon
valley	hill	slopes

What can we find at the playground or park?

Materials
- measuring tools
- drawing tools

Phenomenon Remember that a map is a model. Make a map of a playground or a park near you.

Procedure

☐ **1.** Draw a map of a playground or park near you. Be sure to identify any landforms or bodies of water.

☐ **2.** Have a partner choose two points on the map. Label the points A and B.

Science Practice

You **get information** so you can share what you learn with others.

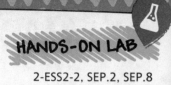

☐ **3.** Tell or write directions for getting from point A to point B.

☐ **4.** Get your teacher's permission. Then have your partner try to follow your directions.

Analyze and Interpret Data

5. Evaluate How easily was your partner able to follow your map?

_____

_____

_____

6. Improve How can you make your map better?

_____

_____

_____

_____

_____

Earth's Processes

Lesson 1 Earth Changes Quickly

Lesson 2 Earth Changes Slowly

Lesson 3 People Can Change Earth

Next Generation Science Standards

2-ESS1-1 Use information from several sources to provide evidence that Earth events can occur quickly or slowly.

2-ESS2-1 Compare multiple solutions designed to slow or prevent wind or water from changing the shape of the land.

K-2-ETS1-3 Analyze data from tests of two objects designed to solve the same problem to compare the strengths and weaknesses of how each performs.

Go online to access
your digital course.

▶ VIDEO

📖 eTEXT

👆 INTERACTIVITY

▶ SCIENCE SONG

🎮 GAME

☑ ASSESSMENT

 **What can cause land to change?**

Show What You Know

What do you think shaped the land? Tell a partner.

STEM Save the Town!

How can people slow down changes to the surface of Earth?

Phenomenon Hi! I am Ms. Williams. I am an environmental engineer. There is a small town on the coast. The ocean is slowly washing away the coastline. The town is in danger!

Help me design a way to keep the ocean from breaking down the land on the coast. Then compare your solution with the solutions of other groups. The path shows the Quest activities you will complete as you work through the topic. Check off your progress each time you complete an activity with a QUEST CHECK ✓ OFF .

Next Generation Science Standards

2-ESS1-1 Use information from several sources to provide evidence that Earth events can occur quickly or slowly.

2-ESS2-1 Compare multiple solutions designed to slow or prevent wind or water from changing the shape of the land.

K-2-ETS1-3 Analyze data from tests of two objects designed to solve the same problem to compare the strengths and weaknesses of how each performs.

VIDEO

Watch a video about an environmental engineer.

Quest Check-In 1

Lesson 1 ■

Use what you have learned. Tell how people can protect a city from flooding.

Quest Check-In Lab 2

Lesson 2 ●

Observe how waves affect the shore and a coastal town.

Quest Check-In Lab 3

Lesson 3 ◆

Design a way to protect a coastal town from wind and water.

Quest Findings

Complete the Quest! How can you save the town? Compare your solution. Present your data in a creative way.

Which Solution is better?

Gardeners need to prevent water from washing soil away from gardens. How can gardeners stop this from happening?

Identify Possible Solutions

☐ 1. Make a plan to design and test a solution that stops water from washing away soil. Show your plan to your teacher.

☐ 2. Choose materials to make a model of a garden. Test your solution. Record your observations.

Observations

Communicate Your Solution

3. **Compare your solution** with others. Tell how your solutions are the same. Tell how they are different.

Materials

• water

• container

Suggested Materials

• loam

• clay

• sand

• small plastic shovel

Engineering Practice

You **compare solutions** to analyze the best way to solve a problem.

⚠️ Wash your hands after the lab.

Sequence

Oceanographers study tsunamis to learn how to predict them. Read about the sequence of events in a tsunami.

Sequence is the order in which things happen. A sequence uses words such as "first," "next," "then," and "last."

Tsunamis

A tsunami is a very large wave that hits a coastline. First, the sea floor moves up and down. This makes the water move, making a wave. Then, the waves move through deep ocean water. Last, the waves get taller as they get closer to land. Tsunamis destroy buildings and roads.

☑ Reading Check | Sequence

Write "1" next to the first event that happens in a tsunami. Write numbers in order next to all the other events that happen in a tsunami.

Earth Changes Quickly

VIDEO

Watch a video about how Earth changes quickly.

Vocabulary

lava

earthquake

flood

landslide

I can provide evidence that fast changes happen on Earth.

2-ESS1-1

Jumpstart Discovery!

Be a volcano. Act out what is happening in the picture. Then act out what you think happens when the volcanic explosion stops.

How do volcanoes change Earth?

Geologists study volcanoes to learn how they change the land. How does the land around the volcano look different after it goes off?

Design and Build

☐ 1. **Design a model** to show how a volcano changes nearby land. Use all the materials. Show your design to your teacher.

☐ 2. Build your model. Observe your model an hour later. Record your observations.

Observations

Evaluate Your Design

3. **Explain** How did your model show changes to the surface of Earth?

_____

_____

_____

_____

Materials
- modeling clay
- large plastic bottle
- white glue
- newspaper
- container

Science Practice

You use a model to explain events in nature.

Volcanoes

Volcanoes are part of the surface of Earth. Many volcanoes are mountains that have a hole at the top. The hole is called a crater. Hot, melted rock called **lava** can come out of the crater when the volcano goes off. This event happens very quickly.

The lava flows down the sides of the volcano. Lava spreads over the land. The lava cools. It hardens into solid rocks.

Literacy ▸ Toolbox

Sequence Tell what happens after lava flows down the sides of a volcano. Tell where the lava comes from. Tell when the lava changes into solid rocks.

volcano

lava cools and hardens

Earthquakes

An **earthquake** is the sudden shaking of the ground. First, layers of rocks deep inside Earth push against each other. Then the pushing causes the ground to shake. Earthquakes also occur when volcanoes erupt.

Earthquakes change the surface of Earth quickly. Earthquakes might cause buildings to fall. They might tear apart roads and bridges. They might cause large cracks in the ground.

☑ **Reading Check** **Sequence** Read the text aloud. Underline the first event that happens in an earthquake. Tell a partner the steps in how an earthquake occurs.

road damaged by earthquake

INTERACTIVITY

Complete an activity on how the surface of Earth changes quickly.

Floods and Landslides

A **flood** is a large amount of water that quickly covers land not usually covered by water. A flood can happen when there is heavy rain for a long time. The water fills up rivers and lakes until they overflow.

Another event that causes a quick change to the surface of Earth is a landslide. A **landslide** is when the side of a hill or mountain falls down. Earthquakes and volcanoes going off can cause landslides. So can heavy rainfalls and floods. Water makes the soil loose. A large section of land may slip downhill.

Identify Circle all the events that could cause a landslide.

Quest Connection

Tell what quick changes could affect a town on the coast.

Prevent Floods

Some cities are in danger from floods. These cities are in valleys or other low places. When there is a lot of rainfall, nearby bodies of water can overflow. They can flood the cities.

Design a Solution How could people protect this city from a flood? Draw your ideas on the map. Label your drawings.

Compare Work with a partner. Compare your solutions.

Earth Changes Slowly

▶ VIDEO

Watch a video about how Earth changes slowly.

Vocabulary

weathering

erosion

deposition

I can investigate slow changes that happen on Earth.

I can explain how wind and water can change the shape of the land.

2-ESS1-1

Jumpstart Discovery!

Look at the picture of the mountains. Circle where the land has been built up. Draw an X where the land is flat. Talk with a partner about how the land looks different in each area.

How do mountains change?

Geologists study mountains to learn how they form. How can you make a model to investigate if mountains change?

Design and Build

☐ 1. Make a plan to model how weather and animals might change a mountain. Use all the materials. Show your plan to your teacher.

☐ 2. **Build your model.** Test your model. Record your observations.

Observations

Materials

- loam
- sand
- pebbles
- container
- safety goggles
- water
- toy animal
- small fan

Science Practice

You build a model to show how events in nature happen.

⚠ Wear safety goggles.

⚠ Be careful using the fan.

⚠ Wash your hands after the lab.

Evaluate Your Design

3. **Explain** Tell how your model showed what might change a mountain.

Earth Movement and Mountains

▶ **INTERACTIVITY**

Complete an activity that explores slow changes to the surface of Earth.

Mountains are part of the surface of Earth. Mountains can be hundreds to thousands of meters tall. The land around them is sometimes flat. Mountains form when layers of rock deep under the surface of Earth push together. This pushing makes the land rise up. Over millions of years, the pushing forms tall mountains.

Use Evidence Read about how mountains form. Then look at the chart. Use details from these two sources. Tell why mountain forming is a slow process.

Mountain	Age
Appalachian Mountains	~300-500 million years old
Himalayan Mountains	~50 million years old

Erosion and Deposition

There are slow changes to the surface of Earth that can take millions of years.

Weathering is the breaking up of rock. Plant roots grow in the cracks of rocks. The roots can break the rocks into pieces. Water and ice can also break rocks into pieces.

Erosion happens when soil, sand, and small bits of a rock are removed. Rain, snow, and wind cause erosion. People and animals can erode rock and dirt on a mountain when they walk on it.

Deposition happens when wind and water drop sand, soil, and small bits of rock in a new place. Rivers drop most of these materials at deltas. These are places where rivers flow into the ocean.

Crosscutting Concepts ▸ Toolbox

Stability and Change
Tell how erosion is different from an earthquake. Tell how it is similar.

Quest Connection

Tell how ocean waves cause erosion. Tell why it can be important to prevent it.

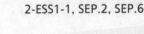
How does the ocean affect a coastal town?

Coastal engineers study how ocean waves affect the shore and coastal towns. How can you observe these processes?

Materials

- safety goggles
- sand
- loam
- pebbles
- water
- container

Suggested Materials

- cardboard
- glue
- tape
- plastic spoon

Design and Build

☐ 1. Design a model to show how ocean waves affect the shore and the town. Make a plan to test your model. Show your plan to your teacher.

☐ 2. Build your model. Test how ocean waves affect the land. Record your observations on a piece of paper.

Engineering Practice

You **define the problem** that needs to be solved.

Evaluate Your Design

3. **Explain** Tell what a coastal town would look like after a few hours of waves. Tell what it would look like after many years of waves.

⚠ Wear safety goggles.
⚠ Wash your hands after the lab.

SOLVE it with SCIENCE

What if slow changes on Earth stopped?

Phenomenon Think about how a mountain and a delta are affected by erosion, weathering, and deposition. Remember that these slow changes are closely related. If one process stops or changes, this affects the other processes.

Use evidence from what you learned to complete this sentence:

If all erosion, weathering, and deposition on Earth stopped,

mountains would

_____

- -

_____

and deltas would

_____

- -

_____

People Can Change Earth

▶ **VIDEO**

Watch a video on how people can change Earth.

Vocabulary

dike

levee

windbreak

I can describe how people change the surface of Earth.

2-ESS1-1, 2-ESS2-1, K-2-ETS1-3

Jumpstart Discovery!

Tear a piece of paper into small pieces. Blow on them. What happened? Now use your hands to make a wall in front of the pieces of paper. Blow again. What happened this time?

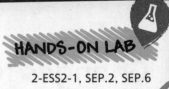
How do plants protect fields from wind?

Ranchers need to keep their soil from blowing away. How can you design a natural solution to protect soil on a field from wind?

Materials

- loam
- container
- safety goggles
- mini ferns
- hand fan

Design and Build

☐ 1. **Design a solution** to show how ranchers can use plants to protect their soil from wind.

☐ 2. Make a plan to test your design. Show your plan to your teacher.

☐ 3. Build your model. Test it before and after you add the ferns. Record your observations on a piece of paper.

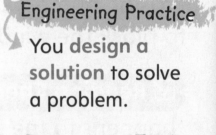

Engineering Practice

You **design a solution** to solve a problem.

⚠ Wear safety goggles.

Evaluate Your Design

4. **Explain** Without a solution that blocks wind, how might the wind affect soil over a long period of time?

_____

_____

_____

_____

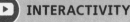
▶ **INTERACTIVITY**

Complete an activity to explore how people change land.

Changes to Land

People making changes to land is a main cause of erosion. We cut down trees. Then we build houses. We make tunnels through mountains. Then we build roads. We dig into the surface of Earth. Then we take out rocks and minerals. Many of these changes we make cause erosion and deposition.

Some of the changes we make slow down erosion and deposition. We build structures to block the wind.

☑ **Reading Check** **Sequence** Tell what happens to the surface of Earth after people make tunnels through mountains to build roads.

Changes to Water

People change water environments in many ways. We drain areas of water. Then we build buildings in their place. We change the way that rivers flow. We build structures to stop floods. We build dams on rivers. The dams bring water to cities.

Rivers deposit eroded soil and rock into the ocean. We take deposited sand from the ocean floor. We do this so ships can pass. Some of these changes cause erosion and deposition. Some of these changes slow down erosion and deposition.

Identify Underline which changes you think people make that slows down erosion or deposition. Read books about Hoover Dam. Write what you learned. Tell a partner.

Hoover Dam

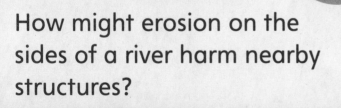

Quest Connection

How might erosion on the sides of a river harm nearby structures?

Stop Wind and Water

A **dike** is a long wall built to hold back ocean water. People build them to make dry land out of land that used to be underwater.

A **levee** is a short wall along a river. People build them to hold back rising water levels. Levees protect farm fields and cities. They are usually made of soil, sand, and rocks.

A **windbreak** is a row of objects that blocks the wind. They can be made of trees, bushes, or fences.

Plants can stop soil erosion on slopes and hills. The roots help hold the soil in place.

levee

Visual Literacy Look at the pictures. Circle the structure you could use to keep water from flooding an area that experiences heavy rain. Tell how you could use the structure.

dike

Math ▸ Toolbox

Solve Word Problems
Levee A is 60 meters long. Levee B is 45 meters long. Which levee is longer? How much longer is it?

windbreak

levee

How can you protect a coastal town from erosion?

Environmental engineers work to slow or stop erosion along shorelines. Erosion can change the natural environment of the shoreline. It can also damage buildings and roads. How can you test a solution to stop erosion?

Design and Build

☐ **1.** Decide which materials to use.

☐ **2. Design a solution** that could protect a coastal town and the shoreline from ocean waves. Draw your design.

Materials

- sand
- loam
- water
- container
- safety goggles

Suggested Materials

- cardboard
- craft sticks
- pebbles
- glue
- tape

Engineering Practice

You **design a solution** to solve a problem.

⚠ Wear safety goggles.

⚠ Wash your hands after the lab.

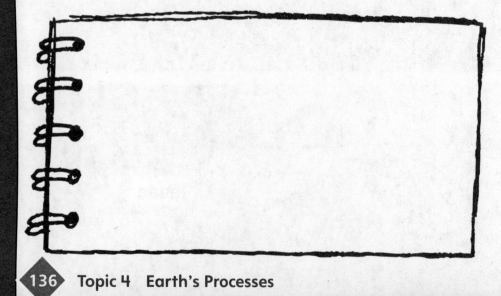

☐ **3.** Make a plan to test your solution. Show your plan to your teacher.

☐ **4.** Build a model. Test how your solution holds back ocean waves.

Evaluate Your Design

5. Analyze How well did your solution protect the shoreline and town?

_____

_____

_____

_____

6. Explain How could you improve your solution?

_____

_____

_____

_____

uEngineer It! — Improve — STEM

Stop Wind Erosion

INTERACTIVITY

Complete an activity where you design a way to protect a farmhouse from erosion.

Phenomenon Construction workers are digging in dirt at a construction site. They need to make sure the wind does not blow the dirt as they build.

Would you like to help them block the wind?

Improve It

The workers set up a long, rectangle fence. It is made out of plastic. The plastic is attached to wooden posts. The plastic has small holes in it. The fence slows down the speed of the wind. It blocks some wind. Some soil can still get through the small holes in the fence. The workers would like to use a fence that does not let soil go through.

How can you improve this fence to keep soil out?

plastic fence

☐ List ways that you can change the shape, size, and materials of the fence to improve it.

☐ Tell how your improvements would stop the soil from going through the fence.

☐ Draw your improved design.

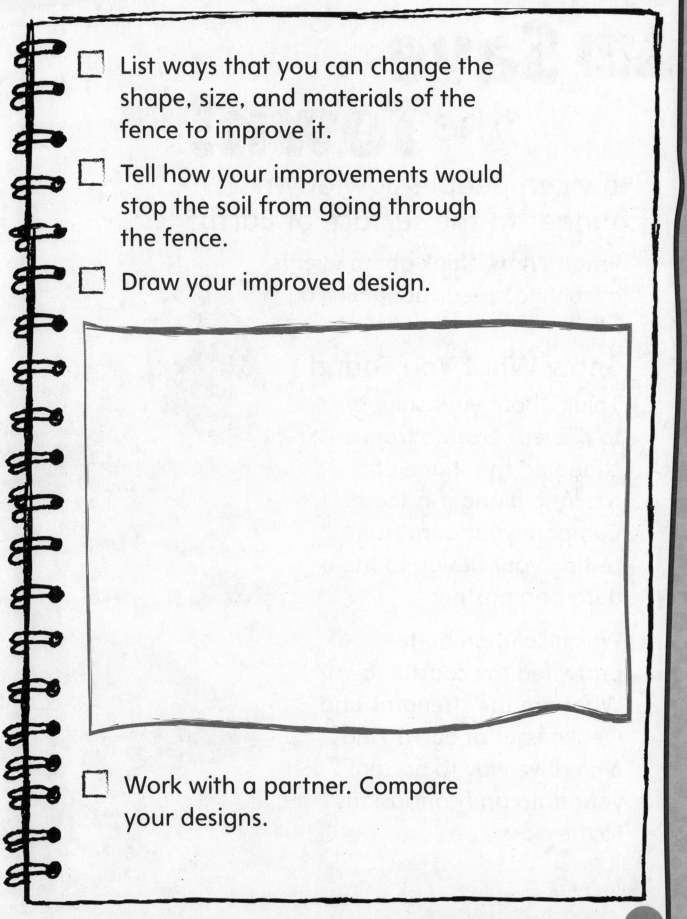

☐ Work with a partner. Compare your designs.

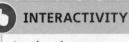
INTERACTIVITY

Apply what you learned in the Quest.

STEM

Save the Town!

How can people slow down changes to the surface of Earth?

Phenomenon Think about events that change the surface of Earth.

Show What You Found

Think about your solution to prevent erosion from changing the shape of the land along the shore. Compare your data from testing your design to the data of a partner.

Which solution better protected the coastal town? What are the strengths and weaknesses of each? Find a creative way to present your data and conclusions to the class.

QUEST CHECK ✓ OFF

Environmental Engineer

Environmental engineers work to fix land and water problems. They design solutions to stop erosion. They manage systems to control water flow. They design systems to manage waste. They monitor air quality.

Some environmental engineers work for the government. Some work for businesses, such as architecture and engineering firms.

What kinds of projects would you want to work on if you were an environmental engineer?

_____

_____

_____

_____

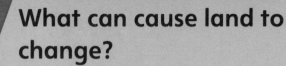

The Essential Question

What can cause land to change?

Show What You Learned

Tell a partner what you learned about slow and fast changes to the surface of Earth.

1. Which of the following is a slow change to the surface of Earth?
   a. volcano
   b. landslide
   c. erosion
   d. earthquake

2. Write what happens when heavy rain causes a landslide.

   _____

   _____

   _____

   _____

3. Name one way that people change the land and one way that people change the water.

_____

- -

_____

- -

_____

4. All of these affect the movement of water EXCEPT
   a. a dike.
   b. a levee.
   c. a dam.
   d. a windbreak.

5. An engineer designs a long, tall dike for a city near a beach. Another engineer designs a short, low dike. Which design do you think is better for holding back water? Why?

_____

- -

_____

- -

_____

Read and answer questions 1–4.

In Nate's city, there are days of heavy rain. A nearby river overflows. Nate sees that part of a hill in his neighborhood has fallen to the bottom of the hill.

Nate watches a news show. A scientist is interviewed. She points to a table that shows events on Earth and how long they last. She says there was a landslide on the hill. She tells about two ways to prevent landslides. One is to cover the ground with sheets of material. The other is to make streams flow away from weak ground.

1. What most likely caused the landslide?
   a. erosion   **c.** deposition
   b. heavy rain   **d.** earthquake

2. Compare the two ways of preventing landslides. Write which you think would work best. Explain why.

_____

_____

_____

_____

3. Circle the word that correctly completes the sentence.

| Weather | Levees | Windbreaks |

_____along the river could protect Nate's city from floods.

4. Look at the information in the table.

Event	How Long the Event Lasts
earthquake	Most last less than one minute.
volcano eruption	Most last less than one year.
landslide	Most last less than three minutes.
weathering and erosion of mountain	Most occurs over millions of years.

Think about what you have learned about events on Earth. Use this evidence and information in the table to describe how quickly or slowly events on Earth happen.

_____

_____

_____

_____

How can you compare different solutions?

Materials
- loam
- small plastic shovel
- water
- burlap cloth
- craft sticks
- glue
- mulch
- container

Phenomenon Engineers test more than one solution to a problem to see which one works best. Think about how water sometimes washes soil away from gardens. Some gardeners put down mulch to slow soil erosion. Some use fabric as a fence to catch soil so they can put it back. How can you test these solutions to see which works best?

Test Your Solution

☐ 1. Make a plan to test the two solutions to prevent water from washing soil away. Show your plan to your teacher.

☐ 2. Build your model. Test one solution. Then test the other solution. Record your observations.

Engineering Practice

You **compare solutions** to analyze the best way to solve a problem.

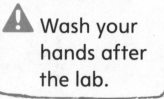

⚠️ Wash your hands after the lab.

Observations

Evaluate Your Solution

3. **Compare your solutions** with the solutions of another group. What are the strengths and weaknesses of each design?

_____

_____

_____

_____

4. Tell which solution you think had a better result for preventing soil from washing away. Explain.

Plants and Animals

2-LS2-1 Plan and conduct an investigation to determine if plants need sunlight and water to grow.

2-LS2-2 Develop a simple model that mimics the function of an animal in dispersing seeds or pollinating plants.

2-LS4-1 Make observations of plants and animals to compare the diversity of life in different habitats.

K-2-ETS1-1 Ask questions, make observations, and gather information about a situation people want to change to define a simple problem that can be solved through the development of a new or improved object or tool.

K-2-ETS1-2 Develop a simple sketch, drawing, or physical model to illustrate how the shape of an object helps it function as needed to solve a given problem.

K-2-ETS1-3 Analyze data from tests of two objects designed to solve the same problem to compare the strengths and weaknesses of how each performs.

Go online to access
your digital course.

▶ VIDEO

📖 eTEXT

👆 INTERACTIVITY

▶ SCIENCE SONG

🎮 GAME

☑ ASSESSMENT

The Essential Question

What do animals and plants need to survive?

Show What You Know

Does this animal get its food from plants or other animals? Tell how you know.

Help Save the Giant Flower

How can you help Mr. Larsen care for the giant flower in his care?

Phenomenon Hi, My name is Mr. Larsen. I am a botanist. I am taking care of a special plant right called *Rafflesia arnoldii*, or the corpse lily. This plant is not like other plants. It has no leaves, stem, or roots. It does not make its own food. It gets its food from the vine it lives on. The flower is about one meter wide, and it smells like rotting meat! Can you design a guidebook to help me care for this giant flower? The path shows the Quest activities you will complete as you work through the topic. Check off your progress each time you complete an activity with a **QUEST CHECK ✓ OFF**.

Quest Check-In 1

Lesson 1

Help decide what the rafflesia needs to survive.

2-LS2-1. Plan and conduct an investigation to determine if plants need sunlight and water to grow.

2-LS2-2 Develop a simple model that mimics the function of an animal in dispersing seeds or pollinating plants.

Video

Watch an animation about a botanist.

Quest Check-In 3

Lesson 3 ◆

Find out what helps the rafflesia reproduce.

Quest Check-In Lab 4

Lesson 4 ▲

Pollinate some flowers in the lab.

Quest Check-In Lab 2

Lesson 2 ●

Decide what should go in your healthcare guide for the rafflesia.

Quest Findings

Complete the Quest! Think of a creative way that you can design a healthcare guide for a plant. Share your guide with your classmates.

Giant Flower This Way!

How are plants and animals alike and different?

When scientists find a new living thing, they record data about it to compare it to other living things. How can you collect and record data?

Procedure

☐ **1.** Observe the images of the sunflower and leopard.

☐ **2.** Use what you know to record your data on the Animals vs. Plants Sheet.

Analyze and Interpret Data

3. Evaluate What do both plants and animals need to live? Tell a partner.

4. Apply Using the evidence you collected, write some of the things a plant needs to live.

_____

_____

_____

_____

Materials

- books about plants and animals
- Animals vs. Plants Sheet

Science Practice

You **conduct investigations** to collect data and answer questions.

Compare and Contrast

Biologists study all living things. Plants and animals are living things.

To compare means to look for things that are similar. To contrast means to look for things that are different.

 GAME

Practice what you learn with the Mini Games.

Living Things

Living things can grow and use food for energy. Plants and animals can both grow. Plants and animals both need food. Plants make their own food, and animals must find food to eat. Some animals eat plants. Some animals eat other animals.

☑ **Reading Check** **Compare and Contrast** Find another reading about living things. Are the important points the same in the two readings?

_____

_____

Lesson 1

Animal and Plant Life Cycles

Vocabulary

plant
animal
life cycle

I can describe some plant and animal life cycles.

_____

2-LS4-1

Jumpstart Discovery!

Look at the picture. Can you find a young living thing and the same living thing as an adult? Tell how the young and the adult are different.

uInvestigate Lab

What is inside a seed or a bulb?

Some plants grow from seeds. A bean is a seed. Other plants grow from bulbs. Explore the inside of beans and bulbs.

Materials

- garlic clove (cut in half)
- lima bean (cut in half)
- hand lens

Procedure

☐ **1.** Look at the cut bulb and the cut bean.

☐ **2.** Find the tiny young plant. Draw what you see.

Science Practice

You **ask and answer questions** to explain phenomena.

⚠ Wash your hands.

⚠ Do not taste.

Analyze and Interpret Data

3. Infer What do you think the other parts of the seed and bulb do for the young plant?

_____

_____

_____

_____

Plants and Animals

A **plant** is a living thing that can use energy from the sun to make food for itself. A plant grows in one place. It absorbs water and nutrients from the soil.

An **animal** is a living thing that cannot make its own food. An animal must eat. Dogs, birds, insects, and goats are all animals. Some animals eat plants. Some eat animals. Some eat both plants and animals.

✓ **Reading Check**

Compare and Contrast Underline how plants and animals are similar. Circle how they are different.

goat

Quest Connection

Tell how caring for a plant or animal may change throughout its life cycle.

Plant Life Cycles

The way plants and other living things grow and change is called a **life cycle**. The life cycles of many plants start with a seed. A seed contains what will become a small young plant.

A seed contains food to help the seedling start growing. A root grows from the seedling. The root grows down into the ground. It gets water for the seedling. The young plant grows leaves. It starts to grow toward the sun. It gets energy from the sun. The adult plant grows flowers that turn into fruit. Seeds are inside the fruit. These seeds start the cycle again.

adult plant

seeds

young plant

seedling

Butterfly Life Cycle

The caterpillar eats many leaves and grows.

Visual Literacy

Draw arrows to show the direction of the monarch butterfly life cycle.

The adult butterfly lays eggs. A caterpillar hatches from each egg.

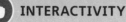

INTERACTIVITY

Go online to learn more about the life cycles of plants and animals.

The caterpillar stops eating and forms a chrysalis.

After ten to fourteen days, it becomes an adult butterfly. It drinks nectar from flowers for food.

Animal Life Cycles

Animals have life cycles. An animal is born, grows into an adult, has young, and dies.

whales

Animal life cycles begin with an egg. For some animals, the egg is inside the mother. The mother will give birth to the baby. A whale gives birth to her calf.

For other animals, the egg is outside of the mother. The young will hatch from the egg. A turtle is hatched from an egg.

turtles

Some animals, like turtles, are born looking like their parents. Other animals, like frogs, look different at birth.

tadpole

Literacy ▸ Toolbox

Compare and Contrast Circle words that describe where a whale's egg grows. Underline where a turtle's eggs grow.

frog

Cycle of Life

Living things, like the rafflesia, have life cycles that include being born, growing into an adult, reproducing, and dying.

Label Write the letter of the description in the box next to the picture.

A. Seed attaches to the vine

B. Flower develops

C. Flies pollinate

D. Seeds develop

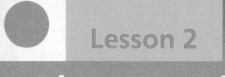

Lesson 2

Plant Needs

VIDEO

Watch a video about how a plant grows.

Vocabulary

nutrient

I can explain that plants need sunlight, air, water, space, and nutrients.

2-LS2-1, 2-LS4-1

Jumpstart Discovery!

Do you or does someone you know take care of plants? Tell a partner something you do to take care of plants.

What do plants need to grow?

Materials
- plants
- water

Biologists make sure plants are healthy and have the things they need to grow. What do you think plants need?

Procedure

☐ 1. **Plan an investigation** to test whether plants need sunlight or water to grow.

☐ 2. Show your design to your teacher.

☐ 3. Set up and begin your investigation. Check your plants each day.

Analyze and Interpret Data

4. **Compare** your plants with the plants of other groups. Tell what you notice.

5. **Compare** how the needs of plants compare with the needs of other living things.

_____

_____

_____

_____

What Plants Need

A plant needs energy from sunlight. It uses sunlight, air, water, and nutrients from the soil to make food. A **nutrient** is a material that helps living things grow. Nutrients and sunlight help the plant make food.

The plant uses the food it makes to grow. Plants that do not get what they need will not grow well. Plants without enough space will be small. If a plant does not get what it needs for a long time, it may die.

Identify Put an **X** on things plants need to live.

Plant Parts

Plants have parts that help them get what they need to make food and grow. Most plants have roots, stems, and leaves.

Roots help the plant stay in the soil. They also help the plant get the water and nutrients it needs to grow. Stems carry water and nutrients from the roots to the leaves. They also carry the food the leaves make to other parts of the plant. Stems also help the plant to stand up. Leaves catch sunlight and air to make food for the plant. Leaves also make oxygen that animals and people need.

INTERACTIVITY

Go online to learn more about how plant parts help plants meet their needs.

☑ **Reading Check** Compare and Contrast Circle three things that most plants have.

Quest Connection

What should a guide about plants say about something plants need?

How can you see the parts of a plant **work?**

Most plants have roots, stems, and leaves. How do they work?

Materials

- celery with leaves
- food coloring
- water
- cup

Science Practice

You **observe** to learn more about things.

⚠ Do not taste anything in the lab.

Procedure

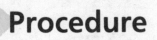

☐ 1. **Observe** the celery and the photo of the carrot. Identify any roots, stems, or leaves.

☐ 2. Make a plan to observe how water and nutrients move from one part of a plant to another. Use all of the materials. Show your teacher.

☐ 3. Conduct your investigation.

☐ 4. Compare your observations with another group.

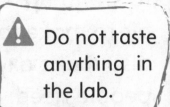

Analyze and Interpret Data

5. **Infer** How is a potted plant like the carrot?

_____

- - - - - - - - - - - - - - - - - - -

_____

_____

6. **Explain** How do you know water moves through plants?

_____

- - - - - - - - - - - - - - - - - - -

_____

- - - - - - - - - - - - - - - - - - -

_____

7. **Evaluate** Why is it important to know about plant parts for a healthcare guide?

_____

- - - - - - - - - - - - - - - - - - -

_____

_____

_____

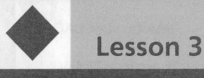

Lesson 3

Animal Needs

▶ **VIDEO**

Watch a video about animal needs.

Vocabulary

shelter

I can explain that animals need food, oxygen, water, and shelter.

_____

2-LS2-2, 2-LS4-1

Jumpstart Discovery!

Do you have a pet? How do you care for that pet? Act like a pet you have or that you want. See if a classmate can guess what that pet needs.

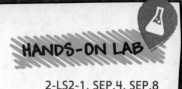

What do animals need?

All animals have needs. How can you meet the needs of a small pet?

Science Practice

You **obtain information** to find out what living things need to live.

Procedure

☐ 1. Think of a pet you have or would like to have.

☐ 2. Consider what the animal needs for shelter, food, air, and water.

☐ 3. Make a list of things you need to take care of it.

Analyze and Interpret Data

4. **Explain** What will your animal eat?

_____

_____

5. **Describe** What kind of shelter does your animal need?

_____

_____

6. **Evaluate** What else will your animal need?

_____

_____

_____

_____

Animals Need Things to Grow

INTERACTIVITY

Go online to learn more about what animals need to live.

All animals need certain things to live. Animals need oxygen to live. When animals breathe air, they get oxygen.

Animals need water and food. Animals eat food to have energy to do things and to grow.

Animals also need shelter. A **shelter** is a place that protects animals. It helps them stay warm when it is cold. A shelter helps animals stay cool when it is warm. A shelter also helps animals stay safe.

Quest Connection

What need do pollinating animals have when they are attracted to a flower? Tell a partner.

Animals Need Space to Move

Animals must also be able to move. Animals may run, hop, walk, fly, swim, or swing from trees.

Animals need space to move. Some animals need a large space. A wolf needs a large space to hunt. Some animals only need a small space. An ant does not need much space.

☑ Reading Check Compare and Contrast How are a wolf and an ant alike? How are they different?

they both need space. one needs lots one needs little space.

wolf

ant tunnels

Attracting Flies

Flies can be pollinators. They carry pollen from one plant to another. This helps the plants form seeds. Just like birds, bats, and butterflies, flies like certain colors and smells in flowers.

Some flies visit some flowers for nectar. Nectar is a sugary drink that many animals like. Flies like nectar from flowers that are dull, dark purple, red, or brown.

Other flies are attracted to the smell of things rotting, like the rafflesia. The flies use the plants for food and as a place to lay their eggs.

Identify Circle the words that describe the rafflesia.

Explain How could flies help the rafflesia to reproduce?

By spreading pollen to other flowers.

QUEST CHECK ✓ OFF

EXTREME SCIENCE

Snow Leopards

Snow leopards live high in the mountains in Central Asia. They live on very high, rocky mountains.

Snow leopards eat other animals. They use their sense of smell to find food. They also leave their own scent. Their own scent is a message to other snow leopards.

In the zoo, zookeepers keep snow leopards healthy. Zookeepers give them high, rocky places to live. They hide food in high places. Snow leopards need to climb to find the food.

Biologists mark trails with smells to help the snow leopards find their food.

Describe How do snow leopards use their senses to find food?

Lesson 4

Animals Can Help Plants Reproduce

Vocabulary

disperse

pollination

I **can** identify ways some animals can help plants reproduce.

2-LS2-2, K-2-ETS1-2

Jumpstart Discovery!

Have you ever found plant seeds sticking to you? Draw what a seed that stuck to you looked like.

uInvestigate Lab

How can you model how animals spread seeds?

Seeds can travel in many different ways. How do some seeds get animals to spread them around?

Suggested materials

- tape
- fasteners
- hook-and-loop fasteners
- paper clips

Procedure

☐ 1. Think about seeds that attach to fur or clothing. What parts do they have that help them hang on?

_____

_____

_____

☐ 2. Choose materials to help you model a seed that can be carried by clothes or fur.

Science Practice

You **develop and use models** to understand how something works.

Analyze and Interpret Data

3. How did your model stick to clothing?

_____

_____

_____

4. How was your model like a seed that sticks?

_____

Seeds Can Travel

Seeds have many different ways to disperse. **Disperse** means to scatter in different directions. Some seeds can float long distances. A coconut is a giant seed that can float.

Many seeds are carried by the wind. Dandelion seeds are light and fluffy. The wind blows them around.

Some plants let their seeds fall to the ground. Other seeds have barbs or sticky materials to attach to the fur of animals.

Animals such as squirrels also carry seeds from place to place and even bury them to eat later. Animals like to eat fruit. When they eat fruit, they also eat seeds. The seeds are spread in the animal's waste.

Predict Why would it be helpful if a squirrel forgot where it hid seeds?

Pollen Can Travel

Pollination is the spreading of pollen from flower to flower. Most plants need pollen to make seeds. Pollen can be moved by wind or by animals.

Animals that move pollen are called pollinators. Animals visit flowers to get nectar, a sugary drink made by the flower.

Many plants need animals such as bees, hummingbirds, bats, and butterflies to carry pollen from one flower to another. Pollen sticks to their legs or hair.

Some bees have special baskets on their back legs for pollen. Both the animal and the plant get something from pollination. The animal gets food, and the plants can make more seeds.

Quest Connection

How do animals help plants make more plants?

What is pollination?

Insects, wind, birds, and bats move pollen between flowering plants. Pollen from a flower's anther travels down another flower's stigma to meet the egg. The flower can then make seeds and produce new plants.

Materials
- lily flower
- cotton swab

Science Practice

You **plan and carry out investigations** to answer science questions.

Procedure

☐ **1.** Use the picture to help you find the anther and stigma of the flower.

☐ **2.** Touch the anther of the flower with the cotton swab.

☐ **3.** Observe the end of the cotton swab. It will have pollen on it. What does it look like?

☐ **4.** Touch the same end of the cotton swab to the stigma of the flower.

fly covered in pollen

Analyze and Interpret Data

5. What did the pollen look like?

6. **Predict** What will happen when you put pollen on the stigma?

7. How does pollen usually get to a stigma?

8. How does the rafflesia spread its pollen?

anther

stigma

uEngineer It! Design STEM

▶ VIDEO

Go online to learn about how a robot bee, RoboBee, can be used to move pollen from one plant to another.

Here's the Buzz

Phenomenon Engineers have built a robotic bee. It is called RoboBee. It will help pollinate crops. After a robot is built, it needs to be told what to do. Write a code for your own bee robot.

Help your robot bee move pollen from one flower to the other flower. Then return it to its hive.

Design It

Write code to help bees pollinate flowers in a garden. You can use numbers, letters or arrows.

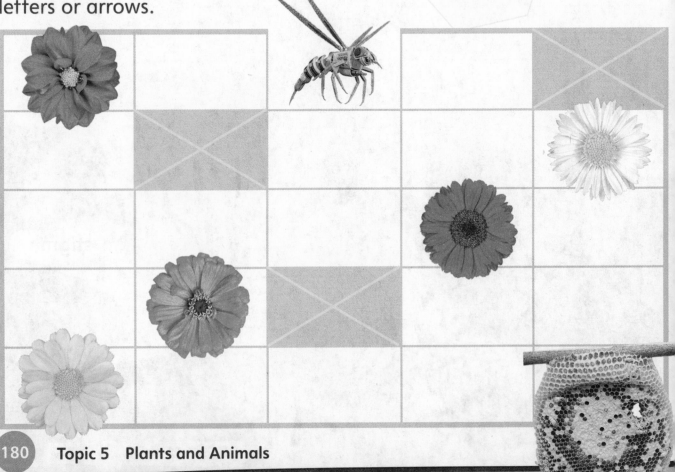

Your Code Symbols			
▶	▼	◀	▲
Move right one space	Move down one space	Move left one space	Move up one space

Your Code							
1.	2.	3.	4.	5.	6.	7.	8.
9.	10.	11.	12.	13.	14.	15.	16.

- ☐ Write your code in the boxes.
- ☐ Use a coin to represent the bee.
- ☐ Place the coin on the bee at the entrance to the flower garden.
- ☐ Have a partner try your code by moving the coin through the maze.

◑ **INTERACTIVITY**

Organize data to support your Quest Findings

Help Save the Giant Flower

How can you help Mr. Larsen care for the rafflesia?

Phenomenon Write your guide to help Mr. Larsen care for the rafflesia or another plant. Use what you know about the things that the rafflesia and its pollinators need to help you plan your guide.

Show What You Found

Think about what you learned about plants and animals in this topic. How do the rafflesia and its pollinators work together to help each other survive and reproduce?

_____

_____

_____

_____

_____

QUEST CHECK ✓ OFF

Botanist

Botanists are scientists who study plants. There are so many different types of plants that botanists usually pick one group of plants to study. They may help farmers learn about growing crops. They may develop new plants that have many flowers. Some botanists travel to faraway places to discover unknown plants. Botanists might even study how plants and animals interact. Botanists are important because we depend on plants for things we need, like oxygen and food.

What is a question that a botanist might study?

_____

_____

_____

_____

_____

_____

The Essential Question

What do animals and plants need to survive?

Show What You Learned
Tell a partner how you can take care of a plant or animal in your home.

1. Where does a plant get energy to make food?
   a. water
   b. sunlight
   c. air
   d. space

2. How does an animal get the energy it needs?
   a. air
   b. water
   c. food
   d. sunlight

3. Draw in the stages of a plant life cycle.

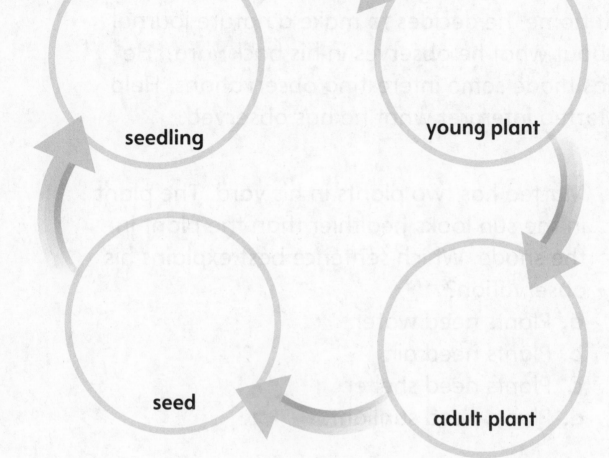

seedling

young plant

seed

adult plant

4. Which sentence tells why animals are useful to plants?

    a. Animals move seeds around.
    b. Animals protect plants.
    c. Animals feed plants.
    d. Animals provide shelter to plants.

Read this scenario and answer the questions.

Matteo is studying plants and animals in class. At home, he decides to make a nature journal about what he observes in his back yard. He has made some interesting observations. Help Matteo interpret what he has observed.

1. Matteo has two plants in his yard. The plant in the sun looks healthier than the plant in the shade. Which sentence best explains his observation?
   a. Plants need water.
   b. Plants need air.
   c. Plants need shelter.
   d. Plants need sunlight.

2. Matteo sees a hummingbird flying from flower to flower. Which sentence best explains his observation?
   a. Animals need air.
   b. Animals need food.
   c. Animals need shelter.
   d. Animals need water.

3. When the hummingbird is visiting flowers, what is it likely carrying from plant to plant?
   a. seeds
   b. water
   c. pollen
   d. petals

4. Matteo notices a strawberry plant in his yard. If animals eat the strawberries, what will happen to the seeds?
   a. They will die.
   b. They will grow.
   c. They will find food.
   d. They will be moved.

5. Matteo sees a large caterpillar hanging upside down on a twig. What will happen next?
   a. It will lay eggs.
   b. It will form a chrysalis.
   c. It will reproduce.
   d. It will turn into a butterfly.

uDemonstrate Lab

How does a plant make oxygen?

Phenomenon Biologists know that plants need sunlight to make oxygen. How can you show that a plant needs sunlight to make oxygen?

Procedure

☐ **1.** Make a plan to show that plants need sunlight to make oxygen.

☐ **2.** Show your plan to your teacher.

☐ **3.** Conduct your investigation.

Materials

- clear plastic bowl
- Elodea
- clear plastic jars
- sunlight
- water
- hand lens

Science Practice

You **plan and conduct investigations** to answer scientific questions.

Observations

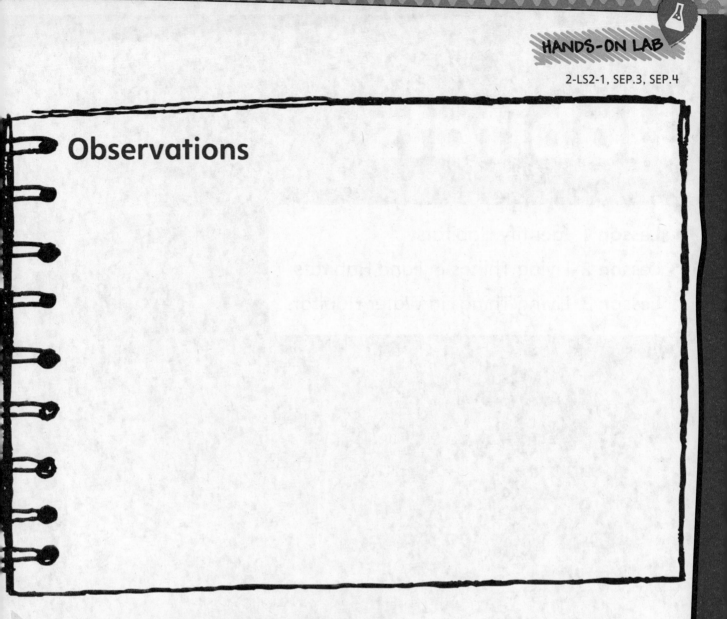

Analyze and Interpret Data

4. **Explain** How can you tell that oxygen is being released?

_____

- -

_____

5. **Draw Conclusions** How do you know plants need sunlight?

_____

- -

_____

Habitats

Next Generation Science Standards

2-LS4-1 Make observations of plants and animals to compare the diversity of life in different habitats.

Go online to access
your digital course.

▶ VIDEO

📖 eTEXT

👆 INTERACTIVITY

▶ SCIENCE SONG

🎮 GAME

☑ ASSESSMENT

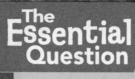

The Essential Question How do habitats support living things?

Show What You Know

Circle the needs of the living things in the picture.

Protect a Habitat

Why protect a local habitat?

Phenomenon Hi! My name is Mr. Rollins. I am an ecologist. I study plants and animals. I study the places they live. I work to protect these places.

I will be talking to city officials. Help me give them reasons to protect a local habitat. You will choose the habitat. You will explain why a habitat is important. Habitats meet the needs of living things. Use what you learn about habitats.

The path shows the Quest activities you will complete. Check off your progress each time you complete an activity with a QUEST CHECK ✓ OFF .

Next Generation Science Standards
2-LS4-1 Make observations of plants and animals to compare the diversity of life in different habitats.

VIDEO

Watch a video about an ecologist.

Quest Check-In Lab 1

Lesson 1

Model a plant with waxy leaves and a plant without waxy leaves. Decide which habitats would be best for the plants.

Quest Check-In 2

Lesson 2

Explore the diversity of two land habitats.

Quest Check-In 3

Lesson 3 ◆

Investigate why some animals live in water habitats.

Quest Findings

Complete the Quest! Find a way to help Mr. Rollins protect a local habitat.

uConnect Lab

What is **out there**?

Scientists learn about different areas by observing them. How can you observe living and nonliving things in an area near you?

Procedure

☐ **1.** As a class you will observe an area near you. How can you observe living and nonliving things in the area?

_____

_____

_____

☐ **2.** Choose materials to use. **Observe** the area. Collect data on living and nonliving things.

Analyze and Interpret Data

3. Explain Tell how many different kinds of living things you observed.

4. Infer How do you think nonliving things help living things in the area?

_____

_____

_____

_____

Suggested Materials

• hand lens

• collecting jar

• ruler

Science Practice

Scientists **make observations** to understand details about something.

⚠ Wash your hands after collecting the living and nonliving things.

Main Idea and Details

Scientists study different areas. Read about the main idea and details of tide pools.

The main idea is what the sentences are about. Details tell about the main idea.

🎮 **GAME**

Practice what you learn with the Mini Games.

Tide Pools

Tide pools provide a home for many animals. A tide pool is an area found on some seashores. The tides fill rocky areas with water. The water stays when the tide goes out. Small living things get trapped in the tide pools. They find the resources they need to survive.

☑ **Reading Check** **Main Idea and Details**

Tell where tide pools are found. Tell how they form. Use details from the text.

Tide pools with water at low tide

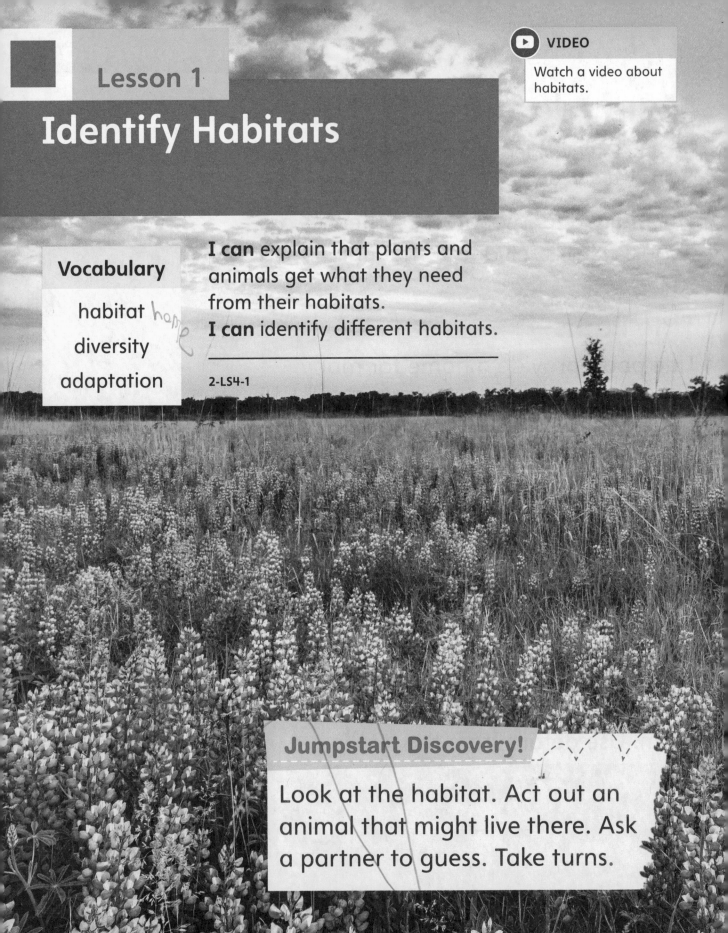

Lesson 1

Identify Habitats

Vocabulary

habitat *home*

diversity

adaptation

I can explain that plants and animals get what they need from their habitats.

I can identify different habitats.

2-LS4-1

Jumpstart Discovery!

Look at the habitat. Act out an animal that might live there. Ask a partner to guess. Take turns.

Who lives in a grassland?

Scientists study which plants and animals live in a place to learn more about the needs of living things. How do living things use the resources in that place?

Procedure

☐ 1. **Observe** the Grassland sheet.

☐ 2. What do living things need to live in the grassland?

_____

_____

_____

_____

☐ 3. Use the Who lives in a grassland? Sheet. Cut out the living things whose needs are met by a grassland. Paste them on the Grassland Sheet.

Analyze and Interpret Data

4. Tell what living things you included and did not include. Why?

Materials

- Grassland Sheet
- Who lives in a grassland? Sheet
- glue stick
- scissors

Science Practice

You **observe** when you look closely at things.

⚠ Be careful when handling scissors.

Habitats

Living things are found all over Earth. They live in different habitats. A **habitat** is a place where a plant or animal lives. Habitats give living things their basic needs.

Habitats can be on land or in water. Some habitats are large. Others are small. The ocean, a forest, and a prairie are large habitats. The soil below a rock is a small habitat.

Compare and Contrast Draw an animal that would live in this water habitat. Tell how this animal would be like other animals in the picture. Tell how the animal would be different from the other animals.

it is the same becuase it lives in the ocean

it is difrent becuase it is called a dolphin

Living Things and Their Habitats

Land and water habitats support living things in different ways. **Diversity** is how many different plants and animals live in a place. One habitat may have many different kinds of plants and animals.

Adaptations are characteristics of a living thing that help it survive in its habitat. For example, fish have gills. Gills help fish breathe underwater. The fish in the picture lives in a coral reef. The fish are colorful. Color is an adaptation. It helps the fish survive.

INTERACTIVITY

Complete an activity about living things and their habitats.

Literacy ▸ Toolbox

Main Idea and Details Read about living things and their habitats. Underline the main idea. Circle one detail.

coral reef

Quest Connection

Describe a habitat near your school or home. Why should the habitat be protected?

Which habitat is best?

Scientists collect and compare data about a plant to learn about its habitat. What data can you collect to learn about the habitat of plants with waxy leaves and plants without waxy leaves?

Materials

- waxed paper
- spray bottle with water
- Leaf Shapes
- scissors
- 2 paper towels

Science Practice

Scientists compare data with other scientists to check their results.

Procedure

☐ 1. Use all the materials. Make a plan to show how water affects a plant that has waxy leaves and a plant that does not have waxy leaves.

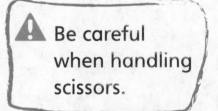

⚠ Be careful when handling scissors.

☐ 2. Show your plan to your teacher. Record your observations. **Compare your data** with another group.

Observations

Analyze and Interpret Data

3. **Compare** What did your data show about the habitats for plants with and without waxy leaves?

_____

_____

_____

_____

4. **Infer** Choose one of the plant types. How could you protect the habitat where it is found?

_____

_____

_____

_____

_____

_____

 **Engineer It!** Define **STEM**

▶ **VIDEO**

Watch a video about planning a habitat to grow plants on Mars.

Plan a Habitat on Mars!

Phenomenon Some scientists want people to live on Mars. Remember that people need food and water. They need shelter and air. Habitats on Mars do not have those resources.

Growing food on Mars would be useful. It would solve a big problem! But plants cannot grow on Mars. There are no nutrients or water in the soil. How can you help solve this problem?

Define It

Now plan a habitat for plants on Mars. Describe some things plants need to survive.

☐ Brainstorm some features that a habitat on Mars would need to have.

It should	It should not

☐ Draw a solution that would help plants survive on Mars. Label the parts of your solution.

☐ Describe how your solution helps solve the problem.

☐ Share your plan with a partner. Tell how your plan would help people live on Mars.

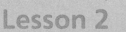
Living Things in Land Habitats

VIDEO

Watch a video about extreme land habitats.

Vocabulary

tundra

I can identify where plants and animals live on land.

2-LS4-1

Jumpstart Discovery!

Look at the picture. Circle five animals that live in this forest.

What do land plants need?

Scientists can model a habitat to study living things. How can you find out what type of habitat is best for a plant?

Materials

- radish seeds
- soil
- water
- plastic cups
- gloves

Procedure

☐ 1. Plan a way to compare how a plant will grow on land and in water. Show your plan to your teacher. Follow your plan.

☐ 2. Observe how the seeds grow for ten days. Record your observations.

Day	Seeds in Soil	Seeds in Water

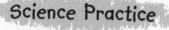

Science Practice

Scientists **communicate** with other scientists to share their findings and ideas.

⚠ Wash your hands after handling plant seeds and soil.

Analyze and Interpret Data

3. **Communicate** your results with another group. Tell what the plants need and which habitat is best.

Forests

Different types of forests grow all over the world. Tropical rain forests grow in warm, sunny areas. It rains often. They are the most diverse land habitat. Other forests have trees with leaves that turn colors in the fall. The leaves fall off the trees in the winter. The leaves grow back in spring. Temperatures change from season to season.

Deserts

Deserts are dry. They get very little rain. Few plants and animals grow in deserts. Desert plants like cacti have adaptations. For example, they have waxy coverings. These waxy coverings help water stay in the plant.

Tundra

Arctic **tundras** are very cold, flat habitats. They are found near the North Pole. They have frozen soil. They get very little rain. They have little diversity.

forest in fall

Analyze Which habitat has the most diversity? Put a check mark next to the name of the land habitat. Tell why you think this habitat is the most diverse.

Science Practice
► **Toolbox**

Plan an Investigation
How would you investigate which land habitat has the most diversity?

tundra

desert

Grasslands

In the United States, grasslands are often called prairies. They are home to different types of grasses and bushes. Not many trees can grow. Grasslands can be cold or warm. Plants and animals that live in grasslands have adaptations. For example, bison have woolly fur that helps them stay warm.

INTERACTIVITY

Complete an activity to compare land habitats.

Quest Connection

What are some plants and animals that live in a land habitat near you?

Habitat Diversity

Some habitats are more diverse than others. Diversity is one reason to protect many different habitats.

Look at the two habitats.

Identify Count the kinds of living things shown in each habitat. Write the number in the box.

Analyze Which habitat is more diverse? Why do you think it is more diverse?

African because there are 6 diffrent animo and fresh water

Living Things in Water Habitats

Vocabulary

wetland

marsh

swamp

I can identify where plants and animals live in water.

2-LS4-1

Jumpstart Discovery!

Circle an adaptation of a living thing in the picture. Tell why the adaptation helps the living thing survive in water.

How do plants survive in water?

Scientists make models of living things to study their adaptations. What adaptations help a plant live in water?

Design and Build

☐ 1. **Design a model** of a water plant. Draw and label your design. Show your design to your teacher.

Materials

- container with water

Suggested Materials

- clay
- gravel
- pipe cleaners
- paperclips
- cork pieces
- aluminum foil
- string
- craft sticks

☐ 2. Choose which materials you will use. Build and test your model.

Evaluate Your Design

3. What adaptations do plants need in a water habitat? How do you know?

Science Practice

Scientists design models to explain how things work.

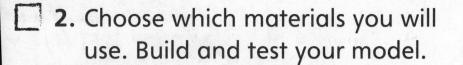

The Ocean

The ocean is a large body of salt water. Some ocean habitats are warm. Others are cold. Some are icy.

Different plants and animals live in the ocean. Some live in the deep ocean. Others live near the surface. Others live near the shore.

Visual Literacy

Look at the pictures. Explain what the ocean habitat provides for these living things.

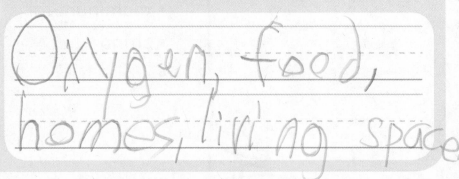

Oxygen, food, homes, living space.

Connecting Concepts ► Toolbox

Structure and Function

The bodies of whales are adapted to live in the ocean. Thick blubber keeps them warm. Large lungs help them dive deep. What are two other adaptations you can observe in a whale's body?

Rivers and Streams

Most rivers and streams are fresh water. Some rivers and streams are wide and flow for long distances. Water in rivers and streams can flow quickly or slowly. Rivers and streams have a lot of diversity, including water plants and fish.

> ☑ **Reading Check** Main Idea and Details Circle the detail that compares the sizes of rivers and streams.

Quest Connection

Would you like to protect a water habitat or a land habitat? Explain your choice.

salmon swimming in a river

⊕ **INTERACTIVITY**

Complete an activity that explores interactions in water habitats.

Wetlands

A **wetland** is a habitat that has both land and water. It can be covered with water all the time or just some of the time. The soil in a wetland is almost always wet. Wetlands have a lot of diversity. Many animals use wetlands to raise their young.

Marshes and swamps are wetlands. A **marsh** has plants that are like grasses. A **swamp** has plants that are like trees. Marshes and swamps may look like ponds during the wet season. During the dry season the soil stays wet.

Compare and Contrast Circle words that describe how a marsh and swamp are similar. Underline words that describe how they are different.

a swamp habitat

Why Some Animals Live in Water

Water habitats provide basic needs for animals that live there. These basic needs include water, shelter, and food.

Water habitats are diverse. Animals that live in water have certain features. These features help them survive in the habitat.

Identify Look at the pictures. Draw an X on the animal that does not belong to a water habitat. Tell why you think this animal does not belong. Tell why you think the other animals belong.

Infer Why do you think it is important to protect many different habitats?

_____

_____

_____

_____

QUEST CHECK ✓ OFF

Add and Subtract

A population is the number of living things in a habitat. Populations change over time. Scientists use math. They calculate the size of a population.

There were 60 dolphins in a habitat. In one year, 32 dolphin calves were born. But 7 dolphins died, and 10 moved to a new habitat.

Calculate How many dolphins are in the population now?

Protect a Habitat

Why protect a local habitat?

Phenomenon Think of all the land and water habitats you learned about. How does a habitat support living things? Why is it important to protect a habitat? Now it is time to choose a habitat to protect.

Show What You Know

Share information about the habitat you chose. Be creative! For example, you could make a video, a poster, or a slideshow. Remember to include important features of the habitat. Explain why the habitat is important. Tell which resources it has. Identify which living things need that habitat.

QUEST CHECK ✓ OFF

Ecologist

Ecologists study living things and their habitats. They work to protect habitats. Some ecologists travel all over the world. Others work in a laboratory.

Ecologists want to know how living and nonliving things interact. They also want to know how living things use their habitats.

These scientists communicate their research to governments and to other scientists. They suggest ways to protect different habitats.

Would you like to be an ecologist? Why or why not?

_____

_____

_____

_____

The Essential Question

How do habitats support living things?

Show What You Learned
Tell a partner how a habitat supports one living thing. Take turns.

1. What resources does a habitat offer to living things?

   _____

   -

   _____

   _____

   -

   _____

2. Label each habitat.

   _____
   - - - - - - - - - - - - - - -
   _____

   _____
   - - - - - - - - - - - - - - -
   _____

3. Draw a line between the living thing and its habitat.

river

desert

forest

4. How is the diversity different in a forest habitat and a desert habitat?

_____

_____

_____

5. How are plants different in marshes and swamps?

_____

_____

_____

Read and answer questions 1–4.

Joe and his family went on a trip. They visited two places. Their first stop was a place that was dry. Joe saw a plant with sharp needles and a waxy coating. It did not need much water to survive.

The second place Joe's family went was cooler. It was also grassy. It had rivers and streams.

Next year Joe's family will go to a different place. It has tall trees. It rains every day. The temperature is warm all year.

1. What type of habitat did Joe and his family go to first?
   a. swamp
   b. tundra
   c. desert
   d. wetland

2. Which type of habitat does Joe want to go to next year?
   a. desert
   b. tropical rainforest
   c. grassland
   d. marsh

3. Write how Joe could tell the difference between a river and a stream.

_____

- -

_____

- -

_____

4. Circle the word that correctly completes the sentence.

diversity   marsh   seasons   tundra

Joe will most likely see more plants and animals next year because the habitat has more _____ .

How can you compare diversity in two habitats?

Phenomenon Scientists learn about habitats by observing them. How can you observe habitats to compare their diversity?

Procedure

☐ 1. As a class you will **observe** two habitats near you. How can you observe the habitats? What materials will you use?

_____

_____

_____

_____

_____

☐ 2. **Observe** the habitats. **Collect data** on living and nonliving things.

Observations

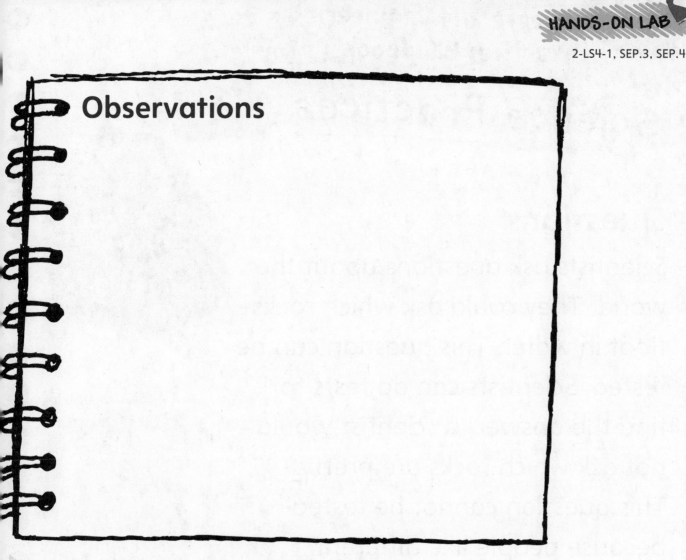

Analyze and Interpret Data

3. **Use Evidence** Based on your data, tell which habitat has more living things.

4. **Infer** Why do you think one habitat has more living things than the other?

Science Practices

Questions

Scientists ask questions about the world. They could ask which rocks float in water. This question can be tested. Scientists can do tests to find the answer. A scientist would not ask which rocks are pretty. This question cannot be tested because people like different rocks.

Ask one question that you have about these rocks. Tell if your question can be tested.

_____

_____

_____

Investigations

Scientists look for answers. They investigate. They do fair tests. In a fair test, you change one thing. Then you see what happens. You could drop a rock to see if it breaks. Then you can try a different rock. But you must drop it from the same height. If you change the height, the test is not fair.

A scientist puts a big rock in fresh water. He puts a small rock in salt water. Tell if this is a fair test. Explain why or why not.

_____

_____

_____

_____

_____

_____

Science Practices

Tools

Scientists observe things to learn about them. What they learn is called information. Scientists can use their senses to get information. They can look and listen. They can also use tools to get more information. They can use a balance to measure weight. They can use a graduated cylinder to measure liquids. They can use a metric ruler to measure length.

Circle the tool you could use to measure the length of the crystal.

Information is important. Sometimes it is hard to remember all the information. Scientists do not want to forget what they have learned. They record all the information that they find. They draw or write what they observe. They use notebooks and computers.

What kind of information could you collect about these minerals? What tools can you use to observe?

_____

_____

_____

_____

_____

_____

Science Practices

Analyze and Interpret Data

What kinds of rocks are in rivers? A scientist would not just guess. She would collect information, or data. She would analyze and interpret the data. You interpret data when you try to understand what it means.

There are fossils in some rocks.

Observe the fossil. Draw what you think this place looked like when the animal was alive.

How to Measure

Scientists can measure very small or very large things. They must use the correct tools. You can measure a pencil with a metric ruler. A grain of sand would be hard to measure. Scientists measure things carefully. They may measure something more than once.

Which tool would you use to measure the fossil? Explain to a partner how to use that tool.

Science Practices

Explanations

You explain something when you help others understand it. Scientists can draw or build a model to explain how something works. A model is a copy of a real thing. When you draw something, you are making a model.

This drawing shows layers of soil.

Draw a model of something you like. Add labels to show how it works.

SEP.2 Developing and using models
SEP.6 Constructing explanations and designing solutions
SEP.7 Engaging in argument from evidence

Arguments from Evidence

Scientists share what they know. They use arguments and evidence. In an argument, you tell what you know. You also tell why you think it is true. The facts that show that something is true are called evidence. Scientists use data as evidence.

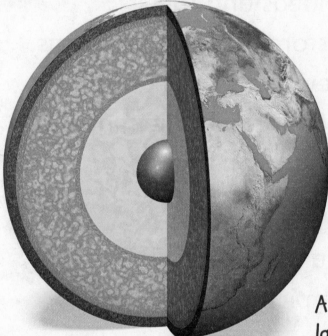

A model of the layers of Earth

Look at the model of Earth. How could a scientist find evidence that the layers inside Earth are hot?

Science Practices

Teamwork

Scientists often work together. They can get information from other scientists. They share new ideas and facts. They brainstorm to solve problems. Scientists review the work of other scientists. When someone makes a mistake, others can help.

Real gold has rounder edges and is shinier than fool's gold.

Work with a partner.
Look at the pictures.
Think of ways to identify
which mineral is gold
and which is not.

_____

_____

_____

_____

Communication

Scientists communicate their work. Sometimes they present their work in person. Sometimes they write papers. Sometimes they write books. They share what they find with each other. They learn from the work of others. They describe what they observe. Scientists also share with the community.

Circle two ways that scientists share their findings.

Engineering Practices

Define a Problem

Engineers try to find answers to problems. Their work helps a community. They start by defining a problem they can solve.

Tell what problem the engineers were trying to solve when they designed the machines in the rock quarry.

machine

SEP.1 Asking questions and defining problems
SEP.2 Developing and using models
SEP.3 Planning and carrying out investigations
SEP.6 Constructing explanations and designing solutions

Design a Solution

Next, engineers design different ways to solve a problem. They test their solutions. Each test is a fair test. They can use models to help them.

This rock contains copper that can be used to make wires.

Copper is used to make wires and pipes in homes. Electricity can run through copper wires. Tell how engineers can test copper wires.

Engineering Practices

Improve the Design

Engineers are always looking for a better solution. They do tests. They collect and record data. They use data from other engineers. They analyze and interpret the data. Engineers use data as evidence. They use it to improve their solution.

Work with a partner.
Tell how you would improve the design of a tunnel through a mountain.

Engineers share their work with others. They review the work of others. Engineers give each other feedback. Feedback is what others think of what you do. Engineers use the feedback to improve their designs. They test their new design solutions.

What tools and information would you use to work on the tunnel problem?

_____

_____

_____

_____

_____

Glossary

The glossary uses letters and signs to show how words are pronounced. The mark ′ is placed after a syllable with a primary or heavy accent. The mark ′ is placed after a syllable with a secondary or lighter accent.

A

adaptation (ad′ ap tā′ shən) A characteristic of a living thing that helps it survive in its habitat. The thorns on a rose stem are an **adaptation**.

animal (an′ ə məl) A living thing that cannot make its own food. A dog is an **animal**.

assemble (ə sem′ bəl) To put something together. You can **assemble** a puzzle by fitting its pieces together.

canyon (kan′ yən) A deep valley with steep walls. It was very hard to climb up the wall of the **canyon**.

deposition (di′ poz i′ shən) What happens when wind and water drop rock and soil in a new place. The river delta was formed by **deposition.**

dike (dīk) A long wall built to hold back ocean water. The **dike** was built to make dry land from land that was underwater.

disperse (dis pėrs′) To scatter in different directions. The wind helped to **disperse** the dandelion seeds.

diversity (də vėr′ sə tē) The different kinds of plants and animals in one place. Rainforests have a lot of **diversity**.

earthquake (ėrth′ kwāk′) The sudden shaking of Earth. An **earthquake** can cause buildings to fall.

erosion (i rō′ zhən) What happens when sand, soil, and bits of rock are removed. The strong winds caused **erosion** of the lake shore.

flexibility (flek′ sə bil′ ə tē) The ability of matter to bend. Rubber has more **flexibility** than metal.

flood (flud) A large amount of water that quickly covers land that is usually dry. The heavy storm caused a **flood** in our town.

fresh water (fresh′ wȯ′ tər) Water that has very little salt. The pond in the park is filled with **fresh water.**

gas (gas) Matter that does not have its own shape or size. Hot **gas** inside the balloon made it rise into the sky.

glacier (glā′ shər) A large body of flowing ice. The **glacier** moved very slowly down the hill.

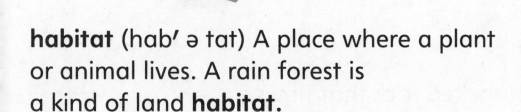

habitat (hab′ ə tat) A place where a plant or animal lives. A rain forest is a kind of land **habitat.**

hardness (härd′ nes) How hard or solid an object is compared to other objects. A diamond has greater **hardness** than any other material.

key (kē) An explanation of the pictures and signs on a map. The **key** showed that green squares on the map are parks.

landform (land′ fôrm′) A feature of land made of rock and dirt. A mountain is the highest type of **landform**.

landslide (land′ slīd′) When the side of a hill or mountain falls down. The earthquake caused a **landslide** on the mountain.

lava (lä′ və) Hot melted rock that flows out of a volcano crater. The **lava** spread down the side of the volcano and covered the land.

levee (lev′ ē) A short wall built along a river to hold back rising water. The **levee** helped prevent the river from flooding the land.

life cycle (līf′ sī′ kəl) The way living things grow and change. A seed is part of the **life cycle** of an apple tree.

liquid (lik′ wid) Matter that does not have its own shape. He poured the **liquid** into the glass.

M

magnetic (mag net′ ik) An object that can be pushed or pulled by a magnet. Some types of metals are **magnetic.**

marsh (märsh) A wetland with plants that are mostly like grasses. Many ducks live in the **marsh** near my house.

matter (mat′ ər) Anything that has weight and takes up space. Solids, liquids, and gases are forms of **matter.**

model (mod′ l) A copy of something. A map is a **model** of a locatiion.

nutrient (nü′ trē ənt) A material that helps living things grow. Fruits and vegetables have many important **nutrients**.

plains (plānz) Flat areas that are often in valleys. The **plains** were covered with short grasses.

plant (plant) A living thing that can use energy from the sun to make its own food. Trees and grasses are different kinds of **plants**.

plateau (pla tō′) A raised part of Earth's surface that is flat on top. We climbed to the top of the **plateau**.

pollination (pol′ ə nā′ shən) The spread of pollen from flower to flower. Bees are important in the **pollination** of many plants.

pollution (pə lü′ shən) A material in air, water, or land that can cause harm. Trash in the river is a kind of **pollution**.

property (prop′ ər tē) A trait or feature of an object you can observe with your senses. Color is a **property** of minerals.

purpose (pėr′ pəs) The use of an object. The **purpose** of using a ruler is to help draw a straight line.

reversible (ri vėr′ sə bəl) To change something back to the way it was. Melting ice is a **reversible** change.

scale (skāl) A way to compare the distance between objects on a map and the same objects in real life. I used the map **scale** to find out the distance from my house to the library.

shelter (shel′ tər) A place that protects animals. The barn provides **shelter** for the farm animals.

slope (slōp) An area that slants up or down. It is hard to climb a steep **slope**.

solid (sol′ id) Matter that has its own size and shape. Ice is the **solid** form of water.

state (stāt) A form of matter. Water changes **state** when it freezes into ice.

swamp (swämp) A wetland with plants that are mostly trees. The water is deep in some parts of the **swamp**.

texture (teks′ chər) How something feels. Ice cream has a smooth **texture**.

tundra (tun′ drə) A very cold, flat habitat near the North Pole. The **tundra** soil remains frozen even in the summer.

weathering (weᴛʜ′ ər ing) The breaking up of rock. The rocks were worn smooth from **weathering.**

weight (wāt) How heavy an object is. The **weight** of the box made it too heavy to carry.

wetland (wet′ land′) A land habitat that is often covered with water. Marshes and swamps are two kinds of **wetlands.**

windbreak (wind′ brāk) A row of objects that blocks the wind. Trees and fences can help form a **windbreak.**

Index

Z

Illustrations

Peter Bull Art Studio; Sara Lynn Cramb/Astound US; Peter Francis/ MB Artists, Inc.; Lauren Gallegos/C.A. Tugeau, LLC; Patrick Gnan/ IllustrationOnline.com; Bob Kayganich/IllustrationOnline.com; Kristen Kest/MB Artists, Inc.; Erika LeBarre/IllustrationOnline. com; Matt LeBarre/Blasco Creative, LLC; Lisa Manuzak/Astound; Precision Graphics/Lachina Publishing Services; Geoffrey P Smith; Jamie Smith/MB Artists, Inc.; Mark Rogalski/Painted Words, Inc.; Mike Rothman/Melissa Turk; Ralph Voltz/IllustrationOnline.com

Photographs

Photo locators denoted as follows: Top (T), Center (C), Bottom (B), Left (L), Right (R), Background (Bkgd)

Covers

Front Cover: Shene/Moment/Getty Images;
Back Cover: Marinello/DigitalVision Vectors/Getty Images;

Front Matter

iv: Clari Massimiliano/Shutterstock; vi: Michael Jung/Fotolia; vii: Dragon Images/Shutterstock; viii: Westend61/Getty Images; ix: Cristovao/Shutterstock; x: Wavebreakmedia/Shutterstock; xi: Noel Hendrickson/Getty Images; xii Bkgrd: Brian J. Skerry/National Geographic/Getty Images; xii TR: Old Apple/Shutterstock; xiii B: Pearson Education; xiii TL: Pearson Education

Topic 1

000: Avalon_Studio/Getty Images; 002: Michael Jung/Fotolia; 004: Roxana Bashyrova/Shutterstock; 005 B: Photosync/Fotolia; 005 C: Vlad Ivantcov/Fotolia; 007: Richard Peterson/Shutterstock; 008 Bkgrd: Andreas von Einsiedel/Alamy Stock Photo; 008 TR: Elenathewise/Fotolia; 009: Chones/Fotolia; 010 BC: Michael Jung/ Fotolia; 010 R: Smneedham/Getty Images; 011 TC: Valerii Zan/ Fotolia; 011 TCL: Pukach/Shutterstock; 011 TCR: Monticello/ Shutterstock; 011 TL: Michael Jung/Fotolia; 012 BL: Robert McGouey/Wildlife/Alamy Stock Photo; 012 BR: Vladimir Wrangel/ Fotolia; 013: Diana Taliun/Fotolia; 014: Leon Werdinger/Alamy Stock Photo; 015: Robert McGouey/Wildlife/Alamy Stock Photo; 016: Ivoha/Shutterstock; 017: Artem Shadrin/Shutterstock; 018 BR: Michael Jung/Fotolia; 018 CR: Dorling Kindersley Ltd/Alamy Stock Photo; 018 TR: Photonic 11/Alamy Stock Photo; 019 C: Dmitriy/Fotolia; 019 TL: Michael Jung/Fotolia; 020: Africa Studio/ Shutterstock; 023: Michael Jung/Fotolia; 024: Michael Jung/Fotolia; 027: Ilya Akinshin/Fotolia; 028 BC: Michael Jung/Fotolia; 028 CR: Tim Ridley/Dorling Kindersley, Ltd.; 028 TR: Nikita Rogul/Shutterstock; 029 CL: Arina P Habich/Shutterstock; 029 R: Michelle McMahon/ Getty Images; 031 CR: James A. Harris/Shutterstock; 031 TR: Itsik Marom/Alamy Stock Photo; 032 B: Ann Baldwin/Shutterstock; 032 TL: Michael Jung/Fotolia; 033 B: 123RF; 033 BL: Natali Glado/ Shutterstock; 033 BR: Iakov Kalinin/Shutterstock; 033 CCR: Nikkytok/ Shutterstock; 033 CR: Artazum/Shutterstock; 034 BC: Michael Jung/ Fotolia; 034 Bkgrd: Justin Yeung/Alamy Stock Photo; 035 Bkgrd: Andy Crawford/Dorling Kindersley, Ltd.; 035 TR: Blue Jean Images/ Alamy Stock Photo; 036 BR: Aaron Amat/Shutterstock; 036 T: Donatas1205/Shutterstock; 037: Tim Large USA/Alamy Stock Photo; 039: Africa Studio/Shutterstock; 040: Lina Balciunaite/Shutterstock

Topic 2

042: Paul Souders/Digital Vision/Getty Images; 044: Dragon Images/Shutterstock; 046: OnlyZoia/Shutterstock; 047 Bkgrd: Tankist276/Shutterstock; 047 CR: Pixelbliss/Shutterstock; 048: Digital Vision/Getty Images; 050: Dragon Images/ Shutterstock; 051: WoodenDinosaur/Getty Images; 052 B: Apiguide/Shutterstock; 052 TR: Sergey Peterman/Shutterstock; 053 BR: Viktor1/Shutterstock; 053 CL: Lydia Vero/Shutterstock; 053 CR: NA HNWD/Shutterstock; 053 TL: Dragon Images/ Shutterstock; 053 TR: Cherezoff/Shutterstock; 054: Independent Picture Service/UIG/Getty Images; 056 Bkgrd: Vikki Hunt/Alamy Stock Photo; 056 CL: Florida Stock/Shutterstock; 057: Dragon Images/Shutterstock; 058 BL: Science Photo/Shutterstock; 058 BR: Valentyn Volkov/Shutterstock; 058 CL: Peangdao/Shutterstock; 058 CR: Ed Samuel/Shutterstock; 059 CR: Yueh Hung Shih/Alamy Stock Photo; 059 TL: Dragon Images/Shutterstock; 060: Christoffer Vika/Fotolia; 063: Dragon Images/Shutterstock; 064 BR: Peter Titmuss/Alamy Stock Photo; 064 TC: Dragon Images/Shutterstock; 065 BR: Ersin Ergin/Shutterstock; 065 TR: ChameleonsEye/ Shutterstock; 066: John Muggenborg/Alamy Stock Photo; 068 Bkgrd: Geoff Brightling/Tharp Modelmakers/Dorling Kindersley; 068 C: Dragon Images/Shutterstock; 069 Bkgrd: Ilkercelik/Shutterstock; 069 TR: Peter Close/Shutterstock; 070: Sheff/Shutterstock; 072: Echo/Juice Images/Getty Images; 074: John Kasawa/Shutterstock

Topic 3

076: Danita Delimont/Alamy Stock Photo; 078: Westend61/ Getty Images; 081: Bcampbell65/Shutterstock; 082: JGI/Tom Grill/Getty Images; 083: Imgorthand/Getty Images; 084 BC: Westend61/Getty Images; 084 Bkgrd: Aleksei Potov/Shutterstock; 085 CR: Ideas_Studio/Getty Images; 085 TR: Victor Maschek/ Shutterstock; 086: Jejim/Getty Images; 088: Westend61/Getty Images; 089: Fotozick/Getty Images; 090: Nevereverro/Getty Images; 092 Bkgrd: Dietrich Leppert/Shutterstock; 092 BR: Tom Grubbe/Getty Images; 093: Ruth Peterkin/Shutterstock; 094 B: Aflo Co., Ltd./Alamy Stock Photo; 094 CR: Westend61/Getty Images; 095 C: Lucie Kusova/Shutterstock; 095 CL: Suzi Pratt/Shutterstock; 095 CR: PixieMe/Shutterstock; 095 TL: Westend61/Getty Images; 096: SGeneralov/Shutterstock; 098: Fstop123/Getty Images; 101: Westend61/Getty Images; 102: Westend61/Getty Images; 104 Bkgrd: Frontpage/Shutterstock; 104 BR: Westend61/Getty Images; 105 B: Shotbydave/Getty Images; 106 BC: Suzi Pratt/ Shutterstock; 106 BL: Ruth Peterkin/Shutterstock; 106 BR: Victor Maschek/Shutterstock; 106 T: Dietrich Leppert/Shutterstock; 107: Hero Images/Getty Images; 110: Inavanhateren/Shutterstock

Topic 4

112: Purestock/Alamy Stock Photo; 114: Cristovao/Shutterstock; 117: EpicStockMedia/Shutterstock; 118: Andoni Canela/AGE Fotostock; 120 BC: Jacob W. Frank/Getty Images; 120 Bkgrd: Sebastian Crespo Photography/Getty Images; 121: Phaitoon Sutunyawatchai/123RF; 122 BC: Cristovao/Shutterstock; 122 Bkgrd: Kedsirin.J/Shutterstock; 123 BR: Welcomia/123RF; 123 TL: Cristovao/Shutterstock; 126: Johnnya123/Getty Images; 127: Cristovao/Shutterstock; 128: Cristovao/Shutterstock; 129 Bkgrd: Terry W Ryder/Shutterstock; 129 TR: PS Photo/

Alamy Stock Photo; 130: FotoVoyager/Getty Images; 132 Bkgrd: Robert Crum/Shutterstock; 132 BR: ImageBROKER/ Alamy Stock Photo; 133 BC: Cristovao/Shutterstock; 133 Bkgrd: Powerofforever/Getty Images; 134 BR: Kazu Inoue/Shutterstock; 134 T: Jarretera/Shutterstock; 135 BR: Vesilvio/Getty Images; 135 CR: Anthony R Collins/Alamy Stock Photo; 136: Cristovao/ Shutterstock; 137: Stephan Guarch/Shutterstock; 138 B: ESB Basic/Shutterstock; 138 CR: Photographee.eu/Shutterstock; 140 Bkgrd: Hoang Thai/Shutterstock; 140 C: Cristovao/ Shutterstock; 141 B: Cultura Creative (RF)/Alamy Stock Photo; 141 TR: Francescomoufotografo/Shutterstock; 142 B: Andrew Roland/123RF; 142 T: Photovolcanica/Shutterstock; 146: Irina Fischer/Shutterstock

Topic 5

148: Yuen Man Cheung/Alamy Stock Photo; 150: Wavebreakmedia/ Shutterstock; 152 BR: Filipe B. Varela/Shutterstock; 152 CR: JustinC/Shutterstock; 153: Design Pics Inc/Alamy Stock Photo; 155 BR: Sumstock/Fotolia; 155 CR: Domnitsky/Fotolia; 156 Bkgrnd: Claire Higgins/Getty Images; 156 BR: Wavebreakmedia/ Shutterstock; 157 BC: Sofiaworld/Shutterstock; 157 BL: Marie C Fields/Shutterstock; 157 C: MarkGillow/Getty Images; 157 R: Jean Faucett/Shutterstock; 158 BR: Will & Deni McIntyre/ Science Source; 158 TR: Ron Rowan Photography/Shutterstock; 159 B: Rruntsch/Fotolia; 159 TC: Rafael BenAri/Shutterstock; 160 BCR: DP Wildlife Vertebrates/Alamy Stock Photo; 160 BR: Vitalii Hulai/Fotolia; 160 C: Angelique van Heertum/Shutterstock; 160 CR: Avalon/Photoshot License/Alamy Stock Photo; 160 TR: Corey Ford/Alamy Stock Photo; 161: Wavebreakmedia/ Shutterstock; 162: Fotokostic/Shutterstock; 163: Darla Krav/ Shutterstock; 165 BR: Wavebreakmedia/Shutterstock; 165 CR: Olesia Bilkei/Shutterstock; 165 TR: Filipe B. Varela/ Shutterstock; 166 B: Ines BehrensKunkel/Shutterstock; 166 TC: Wavebreakmedia/Shutterstock; 168: Toby Houlton/Alamy Stock Photo; 170: Wavebreakmedia/Shutterstock; 171: hkuchera/Fotolia; 172: Wavebreakmedia/Shutterstock; 173 B: Dennis W Donohue/ Shutterstock; 173 TR: RTimages/Alamy Stock Photo; 174: Schuetz/ Blickwinkel/Alamy Stock Photo; 175: Praisaeng/Shutterstock; 176 BC: KV4000/Shutterstock; 176 Bkgrd: Andy Roberts/OJO Images Ltd/Alamy Stock Photo; 177 BC: Wavebreakmedia/ Shutterstock; 177 BR: Juniors Bildarchiv GmbH/Alamy Stock Photo; 177 CR: Anat Chant/Shutterstock; 177 TR: Martin Mecnarowski/ Shutterstock; 178 BR: Ester van Dam/Alamy Stock Photo; 178 T: Wavebreakmedia/Shutterstock; 179: Photos777/Getty Images; 180 BR: Looker_Studio/Shutterstock; 180 C: Tr3gin/Shutterstock; 180 TR: Linda Bucklin/Shutterstock; 182 Bkgrd: Southeast Asia/ Alamy Stock Photo; 182 C: Wavebreakmedia/Shutterstock; 183 Bkgrd: Photoinnovation/Shutterstock; 183 TR: Colin Anderson/Getty Images; 184: Sergii Figurnyi/Fotolia; 188: Owatta/ Shutterstock

Topic 6

190: Ondrej Prosicky/Shutterstock; 192: Noel Hendrickson/Getty Images; 195: Jones/ShimlockSecret Sea Visions/Getty Images; 196: Joe Mamer Photography/Alamy Stock Photo; 198: Georgette Douwma/Getty Images; 199: Noel Hendrickson/Getty Images; 200: Noel Hendrickson/Getty Images; 201 BL: Clinton Weaver/123 RF;

201 BR: Svf74/Fotolia; 202: Druvo/Getty Images; 203: JPL/ NASA; 206: Joyfnp/Getty Images; 207 L: Arildina/Shutterstock; 207 R : Richard GarveyWilliams/Alamy Stock Photo; 208 BC: Noel Hendrickson/Getty Images; 208 Bkgrd: Philippe Widling/ AGE Fotostock; 209 BR: LMspencer/Shutterstock; 209 TL: Noel Hendrickson/Getty Images; 209 TR: Kwest/Shutterstock; 210: Joost van Uffelen/Shutterstock; 212 B: Isabelle Kuehn/Shutterstock; 212 TR: Gudkov Andrey/Shutterstock; 213 BL: Rich Carey/ Shutterstock; 213 R: Bashiri/Fotolia; 214 Bkgrd: Beat J. Korner/ Shutterstock; 214 C: Noel Hendrickson/Getty Images; 215: John Dreyer/Getty Images; 216 BCR: Predrag Lukic/Shutterstock; 216 Bkgrd: Yuriy Kulik/Shutterstock; 216 BR: Life On White/Getty Images; 216 CR: Frantisek Czanner/Shutterstock; 216 TL: Noel Hendrickson/Getty Images; 216 TR: OneSmallSquare/Shutterstock; 217: Alexander Chaikin/Shutterstock; 218 Bkgrd: Youngvet/Getty Images; 218 C: Noel Hendrickson/Getty Images; 218 T: Butterfly Hunter/Shutterstock; 219 Bkgrd: Hero Images/Getty Images; 219 T: Liliboas/Getty Images; 219 TR: FangXiaNuo/Getty Images; 220 BL: Evgeny Kovalev/Shutterstock; 220 BR: Hemera Technologies/ Getty Images; 220 T: Eric/Fotolia; 221 CL: Steve Bly/Alamy Stock Photo; 221 TCL: 123RF; 221 TL: Dmitry/Fotolia; 223: Anton Foltin/ Shutterstock

End Matter

EM0 BR: Cagla Acikgoz/Shutterstock; EM0 CR: Tyler Boyes/ Shutterstock; EM0 TR: Sergey Kuznetsov/123RF; EM1: Ted Kinsman/Science Source; EM2 BC: Evgeny Mishustin/Alamy Stock Photo; EM2 BL: Gjermund/Shutterstock; EM2 BR: Zcw/ Shutterstock; EM2 CR: Karuka/Shutterstock; EM3 BR: Vvoe/ Shutterstock; EM3 TR: Robbie Shone/Aurora/Getty Images; EM4: Adam Burton/robertharding/Getty Images; EM5: Ermess/ Shutterstock; EM6: Snapgalleria/Shutterstock; EM7: Simone Brandt/Alamy Stock Photo; EM8 C: 123RF; EM8 TR: Shawn Hempel/Alamy Stock Photo; EM9: Lloyd Sutton/Alamy Stock Photo; EM10: Alessandro Colle/Shutterstock; EM11 BR: DonNichols/E+/Getty Images; EM11 C: Flegere/Shutterstock; EM11 TR: Zelenskaya/Shutterstock; EM12: Fat Jackey/Shutterstock; EM13: Martin Barraud/Caiaimage/GettyImages; EM14: Alexey Maximenko/123RF; EM15: Jejim/Getty Images; EM16: Photoinnovation/Shutterstock; EM17: Ruth Peterkin/Shutterstock; EM18: Bcampbell65/Shutterstock; EM19: Jeremy Walker/Science Photo Library/Getty Images; EM20: Ivoha/Shutterstock; EM21: Valentyn Volkov/Shutterstock; EM22: Photocay/Alamy Stock Photo; EM23: Tom Grubbe/Getty Images

My Notes and Designs

Draw, Write, Create

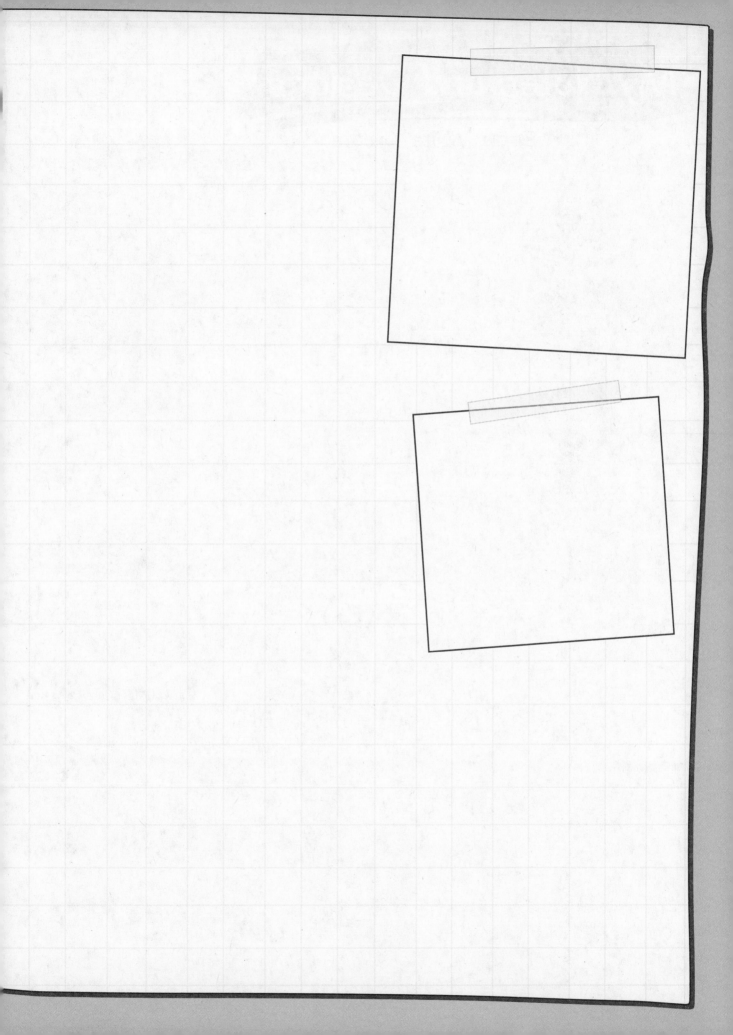

My Notes and Designs

Draw, Write, Create

My Notes and Designs

Draw, Write, Create

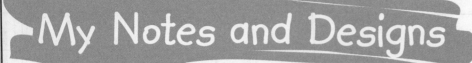

My Notes and Designs

Draw, Write, Create

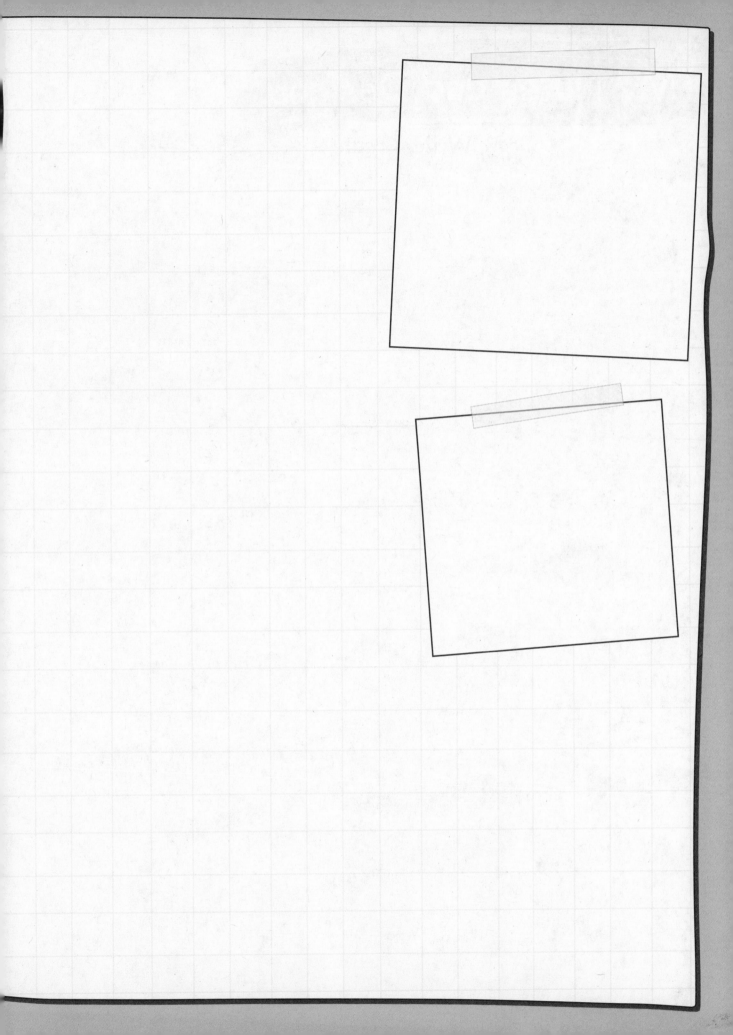

My Notes and Designs

Draw, Write, Create

My Notes and Designs

Draw, Write, Create

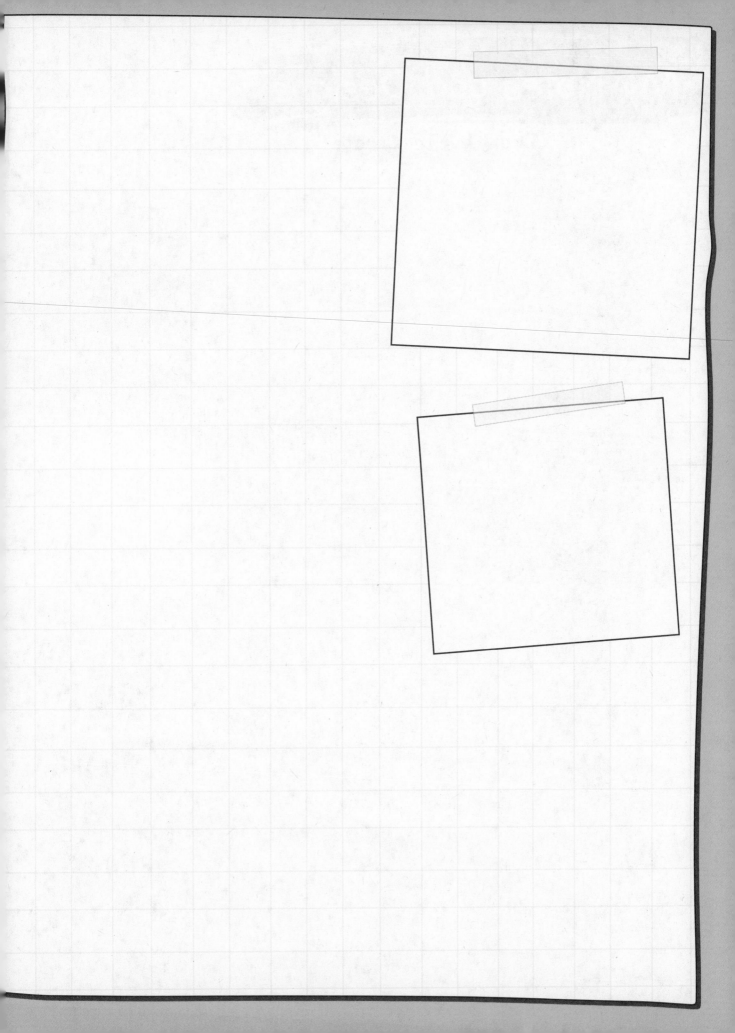

My Notes and Designs

Draw, Write, Create

My Notes and Designs

Draw, Write, Create

My Notes and Designs